HAUNTED
SHROPSHIRE

HAUNTED
SHROPSHIRE

ALLAN SCOTT-DAVIES

The
History
Press

First published 2009
Reprtinted 2012, 2013

The History Press
The Mill, Brimscombe Port
Stroud, Gloucestershire, GL5 2QG
www.thehistorypress.co.uk

British Library Cataloguing in Publication Data.
A catalogue record for this book is available from the British Library.

ISBN 978 0 7524 4787 2

Typesetting and origination by The History Press
Printed in Great Britain

CONTENTS

ACKNOWLEDGEMENTS

Thanks must go to Helen, who helped me put the mountain of notes, letters and cuttings into order and typed up. Also to Henry Manders, Dilys Knight, Morris Kitchen, Malinda Evans, Bob Freeman, Pat Sears, Mrs Colehurst, Droxski, Joyce Jackson, Chris, officers of the West Mercia Constabulary, the late Lord Forrester, the Earl of Powys, the team at the History Press for their patience, and many others around the county who told me their stories, those of their relatives or just good Shropshire yarns passed down through the generations.

INTRODUCTION

Shropshire is reputedly the most haunted county in England. This book is a cross-section of stories from around the county, but there are many more out there and I am always pleased to receive stories to add to my extensive file of cuttings, letters and notes about haunted Shropshire.

There are tales of mermaids, rogue monks, headless riders, kissing ghosts, hanging ghosts, a ghost of a tiger and ghosts putting wrongs right.

My fascination with the subject of ghosts started when seeing a great aunt walking towards the back door of our home in Shropshire. At the same time, the telephone rang and the message relayed that a few minutes before, my great aunt had passed away peacefully at her home miles away. Seeing her so clearly I had rushed to open the door – to find no one there, which upset me more than the news at first.

The stories behind the haunting are often both macabre and tragic, with someone usually having their life ended too quickly, thus leaving the image of them on the screen of time to be repeated during certain conditions for viewers to see as ghosts. My belief is that we all have the ability to see these images, but as we get older and our parents wean us from seeing our invisible friends, we soon forget to 'look'.

It has been a great adventure turning up at haunted sites to check details. I have met those who have seen the apparitions, and sketched the locations – taking photographs too.

So what is a ghost? There are many theories and the one I promote from my own research and findings is that a ghost is a video-type image we see at times when all the elements are right for it to appear. That is why we tend to see more ghosts at night as they are low light energy images that show up better when it is dark. We tend not to see many in daylight – they are there, but are not strong enough an image to be seen.

My theory is that we all have a battery of energy to see us through a full life from birth to natural death. If we die before our natural time, due to murder or sudden accidental death, then we leave a trace image of ourselves powered by the remainder of the 'battery power' that can go on for many more years than if we were alive. Imagine it a little like a projected image through sheets of time, and as time moves on, so fades the image.

The Roman soldiers that walk in the cellar of Treasurer's House, in York, have been getting fainter as time passes. We do not have reports of giant mammoth ghosts, so time plays a part in erasing these images. There are one or two 'ghosts' that do not fit this theory, and they tend to be the destructive ones who are often linked to suicides or young girls becoming young women, with a poltergeist appearing for a short time.

There are more ghosts in Great Britain than in any other part of the world according to the Ghost Club and this could be down to the mix of early invaders from Europe, each bringing traditions and stories of ghosts and ancestors to add to those already told here. Whatever the cause, there are many more stories to be discovered and new ghosts making debuts all over the country, so look out for them.

Good ghost hunting – and remember, it is the living who can kill you – not the dead

one

NORTH SHROPSHIRE

Whitchurch

Civic Centre

The phantom notes of a piano were heard for several nights, drifting from the unmanned civic centre. An investigation failed to find the cause of the noise that can still be heard when the centre is locked up for the night. Nothing has been seen of the pianist in this modern building.

Old Eagles Public House

On 17 June 2005 a group of paranormal investigators recorded the voice of a young woman singing and talking to herself. The investigators did not see an image, but did feel the presence of something in the main cellar where the recording was made.

Wem Town Hall

For many years now, there have been rumours of the ghost of a young girl who haunts the first floor and the back rooms of the town hall. Little did Tony O'Rahilly of Wem think that as he photographed the fire that ripped through the town hall on 19 November 1995 that he would become famous throughout the world. Using a 200mm lens and standard black and white film, he snapped away as fire fighters tried to bring the blaze under control. He went home and the next day sent the roll of film off for development. What came back was to amaze and mystify him. On two of the shots, standing on the fire escape, was a young girl in a long dress with what looked like a garland around her neck, surrounded by the blazing building. He quickly sent the pictures off to the Association for Scientific Study of Anomalous Phenomena, who in turn sent it to Dr Vernon Harris, a past president of the Royal Photographic Society. He checked both the negatives and prints and found 'no tampering of either'. This confirmed that what was in the shots was either a ghost or a very rare freak of light and shade. In 1677, another fire had

The girl in the fire, taken by Tony O' Rahilly of Wem. (© Tony O' Rahilly)

raged through a timber-framed town hall, started when a young student, Jane Churm, knocked over a candle, setting the heavy curtains alight. She died trying to put the fire out. This is still the most talked about sighting in recent times in Shropshire. It has put the famous ghost of Wem Town Hall high on the most viewed ghost photographs.

The Wyke, Shifnal

A number of cottages have been created from the old stable block of Upper Wyke farm and appear to have a groom wandering its length. He is not menacing, but can be a little alarming when he appears in the shower cubicle of the end cottage. This was the old tack room; is he getting a ghost horse ready for the next ride? People have had someone tap them on the shoulder when no one else is around, taps mysteriously turn on and a small boy is sometimes seen crouching in the corner of the yard. The end cottage has a helpful ghost who rattles the household keys two minutes before the man of the house arrives home.

Shifnal

A burgess and businessman of the town decided to have a clock tower built so that the people of Shifnal could always see what time it was, and have no excuse for being late for work. Before it could be finished the burgess was taken ill, and with no hope of recovery he told his solicitor that he wanted the work to stop and he withdrew his funds from the project. After his death the towns' people raised enough money to continue, finishing the clock tower on time. To this day, some people claim to see a white figure jumping in front of the clock dial high up in the tower that faces the main street. Is it the burgess trying to stop the clock?

In the graveyard there is the grave of a young girl who died tragically. Tradition says that if you place a candle on the gravestone and walk round it anti-clockwise three times, the stone slab slides off and the young girl appears in all her beauty to tell you the name of the person you will marry, before returning to her grave with a contented smile.

Nearby is Haughton Hall, which was partially destroyed by fire the 1950s. During the fire, many of the pupils escaped unhurt but their headmistress was seen running from the fire engulfed in flames. She tragically died from her burns, and they later turned out to be self-inflicted, after she poured petrol onto herself before lighting it. A glowing figure is seen running from the rear of the hall towards the lake she never reached, with blue flames shooting from her burning body.

Poynton Green

Two Czechoslovakian pilots died here on 22 October 1941, crashing in the field as they ran out of fuel. A local farmer rushed to the field in an attempt to save them, but was held back by the exploding ammunition and flames. As he looked on helplessly, he saw a large black cat emerge from the wreckage. The cat made its home with a local woman. When she died, the cat vanished, yet appears once every ten years at the crash site.

Child's Ercall Pool

A mermaid was captured at sea and brought to live in the pool at Child's Ercall by her captor, an old sea captain. He treated her well but when he died she was so upset at the way she was treated by his relations that she swam to the bottom of the pool and never returned. It was thought that she guarded the old captain's treasure that was never found after he died. She is often heard singing at the bottom of the pool on balmy summer evenings.

Stanton-Upon-Hine-Heath

At Stanton-Upon-Hine-Heath, the ghost of wicked Madam Browne once roamed the fields, chasing cattle into fences and causing them harm. She also haunted the churchyard, pushing people over and stamping on any tokens left at loved ones' graves. Eventually the vicar called in his friends and they set about capturing Madam Browne through prayer. Surrounding the grave with candles, the vicars managed to catch her spirit in a bottle that was then sealed and buried inside the church. Some years later the bottle was found with a seal of the cross and was carefully placed in the vestry. The young author, Mary Webb, used part of the story in one of her many books based on her beloved Shropshire.

Bomere Pool

Take a walk along the edge of the pool on the eve of Easter Sunday, when you may see the Roman soldier rowing a coracle across the pool that was once connected to a river. He is rowing to find his love who drowned with him as they tried to escape an angry mob who did not approve of the marriage of a Roman soldier to one of the local women. The area is also known for having a wicked community who even corrupted the minister sent to bring them closer to God. On Christmas Eve, one minute before midnight, the minister was drinking and enjoying the pleasures of a local woman instead of reading his sermon from the pulpit. There was a mighty crashing noise and the whole village was engulfed by a flash flood that took them 'to the bottom of the world'. If you are brave enough to visit at midnight, you might hear the minister preaching to the wicked people of his parish followed by the ringing of the church bells as they all try to gain release from their hell.

Sandford Hall

Sandford Hall, near Prees, is an eighteenth-century red brick house. Just before the owner, Mrs Sandford, passed away she told her surviving relatives that she would never leave the hall as she loved it so much and had such fond memories of the joy and laughter her family had shared there. True to her word, she now appears in an elegant coach, drawn by four horses with twinkling lights, along the long drive to the hall. A few who have seen the spectre say that Mrs Sandford waves to invisible crowds with small circular motions of her hand. Mrs Sandford was known to be a keen supporter of the royals and adopted many of their ways, including three square meals a day and high tea. The coach stays within the boundaries of the old estate, whilst Mrs Sandford also appears in the hall on the ground floor.

Beckbury Hall

The small rural parish of Beckbury lies on the Shropshire – Staffordshire border. For over 200 years, Beckbury Hall was the home of the Stubbs family. The most famous of the family, Orlando Stubbs, died in 1869. Orlando Stubbs was master of Albrighton Hunt from 1856–1866, and enjoyed riding through the hall on his horse – much to the annoyance of his housekeeper. Stubbs has been seen riding right up to the front door before vanishing, the sound of his horse's hooves clattering across the hall floor as they go out of the hall and through the back door.

Oteley Park

Situated on rising ground above Ellesmere is the perfect setting for the remodelled hall of Oteley Park. It is elaborately adorned with exquisite carvings in stone and oak and was rebuilt in 1827 by Charles Kynaston Mainwaring Esq. on the site of a former timber-framed Shropshire manor house.

During the late summer months, a woman is seen walking along the shore line up to Oteley Park dressed in a long white robe with a hood. No one has seen her face and the story is that if you see her, dare not to look into her eyes or your soul will be lost. Who is she? No one really knows, but there have been nuns seen in the area for many hundreds of years. Alternatively, is she a past owner, reluctant to leave her home in similar vein to the earlier story of Mrs Sandford of Sandford Hall?

The story of the mere is interesting too. It is said that a Mrs Ellis inherited the meadow with a well where the poor folk of the town of Ellesmere would draw water. Mrs Ellis was so mean that she started to charge villagers one farthing for a bucket of water. The vicar prayed for fresh water to be free for the poor and in answer, during the second night of the ban, the water rose

The gate house at Oteley Park.

up, flooded the sunken meadow and drowned the wicked Mrs Ellis. It is said that if you go down to the edge of the mere on a moonlit night, you may hear the frantic scream of Mrs Ellis as she tries, in vain, to empty the mere.

Little Gadlas, Ellesmere

Dating back to the early 1600s, this small Shropshire long house has had a number of strange sightings – from blue ghosts in the garden (possibly methane spikes from the peat bog) to an old woman seen inside. These disturbances seem to take place when changes have been made to the layout of the cottage. Recently the new owner, Chris, decided to put in a bathroom upstairs that closed off part of a landing. Everything was going well and the work was completed when a watermark, in the shape of a face, appeared on the ceiling of the room below. No leak or explanation could be found. Despite being painted several times, the face of an old woman continued to appear in the new ceiling plaster. One morning Chris was having a shave and nearly cut himself when he saw the face of an old woman looking over his shoulder into the mirror. Shocked, he quickly looked around to find no one else in the bathroom. This apparition has happened twice, and after the second time, Chris decided to shave without a mirror! The ghost got wise to this and now walks the long house with a heavy foot. At the usual time of 3 a.m., the footsteps are heard ascending the stairs, walking on the landing and, after checking two latch door handles, goes to the main bedroom and rattles the latch. The footsteps sound as if on a wooded floor, though it is now carpeted. Chris has followed the footsteps and has seen the door latch rise and the door open by 6-8ins. Bursting into the room, nothing is found. He has two dogs and sometimes they appear to watch someone, or something, walk across rooms. Nothing has been found in the records of the house as to why this spectre appears, but she is witnessed by many others who visit the house. Chris is a down-to-earth horticulturalist who does not 'see' things and I feel we can take his word on this haunting.

Lilleshall Abbey

The Lilleshall Abbey ruins are managed by English Heritage and open to the public in season. It was founded in 1148 for Augustinian canons.

In the 1930s. a young boy who lived in Abbey Cottage lost a lot of sleep due to the strange noises he heard in his room, noises he described as someone turning the page of a large book. A medium called Mr Williams read about the boy and travelled to meet him. With a companion, Mr Williams stayed with the family for supper and went to the boy's room. Disappointed, as he was unable to pick up anything, he heard from the custodian that visitors had reported seeing a monk in the ruins, and they decided to spend the night there. The custodian took them to the spot where a spiritualist claimed to have met, and spoken with, a monk. She could not understand his replies, which were in a foreign tongue. The two waited in the ruins on a still, moonlit night. After two hours they heard the sound of faint footsteps on the gravel. They looked but could not see anything. Some forty minutes later, they heard fifty-three footsteps, and again an hour later exactly the same number of footsteps. No matter how much they looked, they could not explain the footsteps. They waited until dawn to go back to the cottage. Over breakfast, the custodian told them of some of the other sightings in the cottage and at the Abbey.

When they first arrived at Lilleshall the custodian and his wife were met by a young couple walking down the narrow stairs towards them. They were dressed in what looked like Sunday best, with no expression on their faces… they looked, and felt, dead. The custodian asked around the village to see if he could find out who the couple were. An older resident remembered that many years before she was born, and the cottage newly built, a young couple had moved in after getting married in the village. There was much excitement as the couple had just gained work with the Squire at the nearby Lilleshall Hall. When they did not arrive at the hall for work, a junior member of the household staff was sent to the cottage to fetch them. Since they were on their honeymoon, the Squire was not too worried about their absence. Banging on the front door he found it unlocked and walked in, shouting their names. Upstairs he found them still in bed and a faint smell of coal smoke in the room. He tried to wake them, only to realise they were dead. He rushed back to the hall and summoned help. It would seem that the coal they had used in the bedroom had given off a deadly poisonous gas.

Another story was of a past custodian who lived alone with his Jack Russell dog. He often walked the ruins at night to give them both a stretch of legs before going to bed. On one occasion he saw a figure kneeling in the area, 6ft from the east window. His dog had her hackles up and started to bark. When challenged, the person stood up and walked through a door opening. Despite looking, he found no sign of the intruder. The next morning he again saw the figure. This time the man stood up and walked towards him. He was a monk in a black Augustinian robe who asked, 'Do you know the secret of Lilleshall Abbey?' 'What secret?' he asked. 'You will know when the time is ripe' came the reply. He never did find out the secret, as he retired soon after that encounter and was never to return alive.

The Bear Hotel, Hodnet

In the early seventeenth century, a very rich gentleman named Jasper spent many days at the hotel on his way from London to Chester. Jasper was wealthy and fond of the owners' family, treating them as his own, bestowing gifts and favours. Jasper suddenly stopped visiting. When he finally did return, he looked bedraggled but continued to live the life he had always done. A day or two later, with no change of clothes, he told the landlord that he had lost his fortune to a crook who had taken him to see a new venture abroad. Having trusted the man with all his money, bar a few pounds, he was shocked when he was arrested and deported back to England. He threw himself on the mercy of the landlord and even offered to work for his keep. The landlord, it seems, only liked Jasper for his money and was quick to throw him out into the cold, snowy night. As he left, Jasper said he would have his revenge. When his wife and children heard what their father had done to Jasper, they all went to find him but were driven back by the heavy snow storm. That night the landlord was found dead in the seat where Jasper had liked to sit. The landlords face was distorted with terror. In the late afternoon, the frozen body of Jasper was found under a hedge, just yards from the hotel. The family paid to have him buried in the local church, but far away from the landlord. Not long after he passed away, Jasper was seen by every living member of the family waving a cheery hand. He is still seen in the hotel walking the hallways and sitting in his fireside chair.

The Bear Hotel from the Church.

The Corbet Arms, Market Drayton

During the nineteenth century, a young chambermaid fell in love with a handsome travelling salesman who often stayed at the Corbet Arms. Being a young innocent, she fell for his charms and they became a couple. Whenever he visited he promised to take her away with him to get married. She had no family and worshipped her beau. Some months later his visits became less frequent and then, without explanation, stopped. She had been feeling unwell for a month or two and went to see a doctor, who told her she was pregnant. The news threw the young woman into panic. An unmarried pregnant woman was not the type of woman employers wanted and she kept the truth from her boss for as long as she could. One day she was seen in her underwear and the whistle blown about her condition. She was called all manner of names and dismissed from employment. She had one hour to pack her bags and leave.

Except for the workhouse, the Corbet Arms was the only place she had known. Realising that her beau had abandoned her, she went upstairs to Room 7 and took her own life. She left a note to her boss forgiving him and the staff, and one for her lover which was never collected.

Male guests in Room 7 often have the bedclothes pulled off them at night and sense someone standing at the bottom the bed. Some report having their bottom pinched or feel someone kissing them on the lips as they leave the room. Some women have reported seeing the girl hanging from the beam. She is known to take rings from rooms which are later found in the cellar, where one of the owners has seen her smiling to herself and holding a small baby. Her footsteps are heard in the ballroom and on the back stairs.

Moreton Corbet Castle

The brick and stone castle seen today was originally an eleventh-century timber manorial complex, founded by the Toret family in 1200. Originally a stone enclosure castle, Bartholomew Toret added a three-storey square keep and an east range to the triangular moat platform. In the mid-thirteenth century Richard Corbet encased the castle with a curtain wall, flanked by a two-storey gatehouse and in the mid- to late sixteenth century, the Corbet family remodelled the castle into an ambitious Elizabethan Italian mansion which was badly damaged during the Civil War.

The ghost is that of Paul Holmyard, a Puritan who was befriended by Sir Vincent Corbet. As a neighbour, Paul Holmyard took kindly to his offer of friendship and security after officials from London seized his home. Sir Vincent grew weary of his guest, who was becoming more fanatical by the day. Fearing that his home would be next to be seized, he ordered Paul Holmyard out of Moreton Corbet and he left with only a few items of clothing, a little money and some food.

For years Holmyard lived in the nearby woods. As he grew older and weaker, he felt he needed to return to Moreton Corbet Castle. Upon meeting Sir Vincent, Holmyard cursed him thus:

Moreton Corbet Castle.

Woe unto thee, hard hearted man, the Lord has hardened thy heart as he hardened the heart of the pharaoh, to thine own destruction. Rejoice not in thy riches, not in monuments of thy pride, for neither thou, nor thy children, nor shall thy children's children inhabit these halls. They shall be given up to desolation; snakes, vipers and unclean beasts shall make it their refuge, and thy home shall be full of doleful creatures.

Before Sir Vincent could reply, Holmyard turned his back on him and walked into the dark. The next morning he was found dead, huddled under a hedge not far from the castle. To this day, the ragged ghost of Paul Holmyard wanders the ruins of the castle – perhaps to make sure the castle remains a ruin.

Whittington Castle

Built in AD 845 by the Welsh Prince Ynyr ap Cadfarch, it was seized by Roger de Montgomery during the Battle of the Marches and given to Sir William Peveril of Peak. When his young daughter, Mellet, wanted to marry, the challenge was put out to the bravest knights in the land, with Whittington Castle and estate as the dowry. Guarine de Metze, Sheriff of Shropshire, won the contest, wife and castle. Their descendants held the castle for over 400 years.

In the twin towers of this once proud castle, the cries of children are often heard, and they are seen peering out of a small upstairs room. The story behind the haunting is that the heir to the estate had been playing with a cousin in and around the castle when they disappeared. The family searched high and low for weeks until the grizzly discovery of the remains of two small boys were found in a large wooden trunk high up in the tower. Since then the Elizabethan chest has been locked away for fear that if it were to be opened again, another member of the family would die. So much fear surrounds the chest that when it was sent away for restoration it was never opened and is now hidden in a secret location.

Whittington Castle.

The graveyard of the castle at
Ruyton-XI-Towns.

Ruyton-XI-Towns

Ruyton-XI-Towns were created in a royal charter in 1310 from eleven small hamlets that
surrounded Ruyton.

A walk to the church is no real challenge unless it is approaching midnight. The distant
toll of midnight rings out from the clock and at this time it is said that a mist rolls up and
into the churchyard and settles over the remains of Ruyton castle. A headless horseman can
be seen riding towards the old castle before disappearing through the ever-thickening mist
ahead of him.

One of the eleven townships which make up Ruyton is that of Coton. Coton Hall was
owned at one point by Corbet Kynaston, who haunted the hall until 1788 when the family,

fed up with the noise and disturbances caused by the ghost, called in help from Reverend David Evans. He decided to put Corbet to rest once and for all and armed with candles, a bottle and stopper, a Bible and five other ministers, he entered the hall and they began to pray. Within minutes the disturbances began and continued though the day, gradually becoming quieter and weaker. Eventually, just before midnight, the spirit of Corbet Kynaston was forced, through prayer, into the bottle which was sealed with a stopper. The sign of the cross was pressed in wax to mark the bottle which was carried to the nearby pool. There the ministers prayed and threw the bottle into the pool. Water is said to be the one place a ghost will not haunt. This is why ghosts are not often seen close to water. Corbet was laid to rest for 1,000 years. At the turn of the twentieth century some people believed that he had escaped his entrapment and was out and about early; milk churns were pushed off the collection stand into the road and rolled about by invisible hands, and a bush at the side of the pool burst into blue flames.

Chetwynd, Near Newport

The Chetwynd Park estate lies in the small village of Chetwynd on the outskirts of Newport and has a history that can be traced back to Leofric, Earl of Mercia until 1050. Throughout the years the building was remodelled, burnt down and rebuilt in the present form in 1964.

The ghost of the hall is that of Madam Pigott, who married her husband for love only to find out that he married her for her wealth. The marriage was a very cold and loveless one, so when Madam Pigott became pregnant, there were rumours that the child was not her husband's. It was, but he still treated her with utter contempt. The birth was long and painful and the doctor gave the husband the stark choice of saving his wife or his child. He barely hesitated, ordering the doctor that the child must be saved, and to hell with his wife. The doctor did save the child and as Madam Pigott lay bleeding to death, she cursed the hall and her husband, falling silent as she looked at her baby boy.

The little boy died after just three days and was buried with his mother. He was never christened and that is why, the local saying goes, Madam Pigott cannot rest until she finds her son who is lost in limbo. Seen on the locally named Pigott Hill, sitting on a gnarled tree and walking towards the hall in pain, arms outstretched, looking for her son, Madam Pigott screams in some of the hall rooms. Sometimes she has caused a motorist to swerve on part of the Newport road, known as Windy Oaks, to avoid the tall, dark figure of a woman walking towards the hill.

A local vicar and eleven other churchmen managed to get the restless spirit of Madam Piggott into a bottle through prayer and holding of blessed candles but alas, she escaped when the pool into which they threw the bottle was being dredged and it broke open – releasing the ghost once more.

Wild Kynaston, Nesscliffe

Nesscliffe is a small village. The old Roman road, now the A5, runs through the village whilst a new road bypasses it and the nearby British Army base. A short walk from the village are the infamous caves that were once home of highwayman Wild Humphrey Kynaston. He had been thrown out of the family home due to his appetite for drink, gambling and loose women. The family had covered so much of his debt they nearly went bankrupt themselves. Kynaston was unable to meet the debts and was outlawed. This meant that he had no protection from the law of the land. Out on his own, he made his home in the caves at Nesscliffe where he had played as a boy. From here, he would rob people who passed along the road below to Shrewsbury. To confuse his pursuers, Kynaston had the shoes of his horse put on backwards.

One legend tells of an ambush that was set up near the old wooden bridge at Montford. A number of wooden planks were removed by order of the Under Sheriff who, with his men, were in waiting for Kynaston. Sensing something was wrong because the toll keeper was nowhere to be seen, Kynaston galloped towards the bridge, pushing through the line of soldiers who jumped out in front of him. He made it over the wide gap but a rider following plunged in to the River Severn. The locals were so impressed by the jump that they went to Knockin Heath, where they marked the distance jumped by cutting a large H at the start of the leap, and a large K at the point of impact at the other side. They even had a pot of money for anyone who could beat the leap – and no one ever has. Kynaston's horse was named Beelzebub – the horse of the Devil.

Not long after the incident, the ever-confident and assured Kynaston went to his favourite inn of the village and found a stranger sitting in his seat. He went over to him, drew out a pistol and shot the man before calmly drinking his brandy and escaping up a chimney. Following this, there is no mention of Kynaston until a journal records that a Homffray Kynaston and Thomas Trentham from Shropshire entered France in the service of the King on 16 June 1513. Perhaps this would explain why, in 1516, he was given a full pardon from King Henry VIII.

Wild Kynaston
shoots again.

Kynaston retired to a small estate near Welshpool where he died in 1534, leaving a large bequest to the church of St Mary's in Welshpool where he was buried to the right of the chancel.

Should you be out near the field study centre at Montford Bridge, look out for Kynaston, riding Beelzebub, leaping the River Severn in a blaze of fire and smoke. They are seen around the cave and should you be foolish enough to dare to sit in his chair at the Old Three Pigeons Inn you may get a rude start; Kynaston is likely to give you a shove – but at least he does not shoot you!

Nearby Nesscliffe is the Army training camp that used to house many National Service recruits and where strange goings-on have been reported in the local newspaper, the *Shropshire Star*. One young recruit, Mr Manders, told of how he was on night patrol when he heard a noise coming towards him. He shone his torch in the direction of the noise but saw nothing – yet the noise got closer. He shouted 'Who goes there? Stop'. The noise, described as a low level hum, continued. Mr Manders suddenly felt sick and took hold of the side of a nearby hut. Hearing the commotion a number of others on patrol that night rushed to find an ashen Mr Manders shaking from head to toe. Two days later he heard the noise again when inside a hut. Looking out, he and two others saw tall blue figures in pointed hats whirl through the gap between the huts. They rushed out to see who they were, but saw nothing. Even today there have been sightings of the strange, tall, blue electric ghosts. One explanation is that they are no more than methane flames ignited when people have a crafty cigarette – though no one can explain the origin of the methane.

Chirbury Church

Are you brave enough to visit Chirbury Church at night on Hallowe'en? It is said that if you walk twelve times anti-clockwise around the church at dusk on this night and wait until midnight by the large entrance doors, you will hear a roll call of all the parishioners who will die before the next Hallowe'en.

On Hallowe'en 1788, two men had been to the local hostelry and decided they would find out who was going to die. In their drunken stupor they planned to run up debts with whoever was named in the knowledge that it would not be collected. They walked around the church twelve times anti-clockwise and staggered to the doors. They started to hear mumbled names. One name made them sit up. It was their best friend and brother to one of them. They rushed to his home and woke him at two o'clock in the morning. He was not best pleased and told them to go home – he had no intention of dying. But die he did, just a week later, and was buried after a service by Parson Williams, who served the parish from 1787-1808.

Local tradition says that a soul buried in the graveyard at Chirbury does not find rest until it has told a living person of the next one to join them in the graveyard. So beware when walking around the church in case you hear your own name called.

Bull of Bagbury

At Hyssington, on the borders of Shropshire and Montgomery, is the most riotous phantom of the whole county.

The story is that a wicked Squire lived at Bagbury Hall. He oppressed his staff and refused to give them beer (which was always part of their wage at the time). He was only known for two good deeds; the one most remembered is when, in a moment of weakness, he gave bread and cheese to a young boy who had walked to the hall to find his father.

After his death his spirit could not rest and he returned to Bagbury as an enormous bull. He would roar so loud that windows and shutters flew open, terrifying the new owners. The spirit caused so much trouble that twelve priests were called in to exorcise and put the bull to rest. They surrounded the bull, a candle and prayer book in hand, and forced the spirit into the churchyard and on into the church. Here they prayed for the soul of the Squire. Suddenly eleven of the candles were blown out and the bull started to grow in size, so much so that he started to crack the roof and walls. It was the intervention of a blind parson with his single candle that remained glowing sufficiently to give light to the rest of the group, who relit their candles, and continued their exorcism. The bull shrank to the point where they were able to fit it into a snuff box. As the lid was being closed they heard the Squire saying that he wanted to be placed under the bridge at Bagbury so that he could curse every woman that passed to lose her child and every mare to lose her foal. The lid was closed and sealed with wax from each candle, placed in another container that was again sealed and sent off to the Red Sea, where it was thrown in with a large lead weight attached.

Minsterley Hall

William Thynne, Chaucer's first editor who printed the first complete edition of Chaucer's collected works in 1532, resided at Minsterley Hall. It is a fine example of a timber-framed, black and white medieval building. A poltergeist resides at Minsterley Hall and throws objects, from stones to crockery, around the rooms and bangs windows from outside when guests are sitting down for a meal. At one such party, on New Year's Eve, the long case clock struck 11.15 p.m. Everything on the tables, including food-laden silver plates, charged glasses and even salt and pepper shakers flew into the air and dropped to the ground. In the commotion that followed, nothing was broken except for glasses of champagne dropped by guests in fright. Soon after, great noises could be heard as if Minsterley Hall was being ransacked. Upon investigation by the brave servants, nothing was out of place.

two

MID-SHROPSHIRE

Pimley Manor

Pimley Manor has a famous white lady who the present owner, Mr Freeman, met soon after moving into the Manor on 14 December 1963. He had finally managed to get to sleep in their new home when, at 3 a.m., he and his wife Dorothy were awoken by a dreadful wind and whistling in the chimney. 'I am sure I can hear someone walking upstairs' she said to her husband, who went to investigate. When he opened the door to an upper room he found himself in the presence of a poised and beautiful lady, dressed all in white. Most people would turn and run at this moment, but Mr Freeman said that he did not feel frightened at all. He remembers they had some kind of conversation before the lady in white indicated she should leave. She then disappeared through a little door, rather like Alice in Wonderland. The next day he investigated the small door and discovered a trap door in the little room behind. Dorothy insisted this was sealed up. Mr Freeman twice travelled to fetch the midwife for the birth of his son and daughter; the White Lady travelled with him in the car on both occasions. Later, Mr and Mrs Freeman were out walking along the riverbank near Pimley Manor. Turning a corner, Mr Freeman came across a beautiful white swan and managed to get close enough to stroke and talk to it. He looked up and noticed his wife had turned back, heading toward Pimley. He caught up with her. In a rather annoyed voice she asked, 'Why ever did you stay so long talking to that woman, what did she want?' 'What woman?' he replied. 'Why, the lady in white' she said. Since that day he has not encountered the White Lady.

Some time later Mr Freeman investigated the story behind the ghost. He found out that she had lived at Pimley with her twenty-year-old daughter and became known as the White Lady since she invariably dressed in white, rode side-saddle on a white horse and had a white stable – in fact, everything possible was white. They lived happily for a few years until the daughter vanished. The local rumour was she had run off with the groom who was deemed, by her mother, to be below her class. Her mother became a recluse, the horse was sold and the property fell into decline. After her mother died, efforts were made to find the white lady and a sad tale of poverty and untimely death was uncovered.

As there were no direct descendants the property was given over to a local vicar and his family who were distant relations. After the Reverend Scott moved in to Pimley Manor, things started to go wrong. He saw choirboys walking in the garden, faces at the windows, and when he pointed out the window in question to the estate manager, he was informed that would be an impossibility, as the window was a ghost window – real glass and frame on the outside but no corresponding window inside the Manor. He felt a lady dressed in white was watching him and became distracted. He went to the ruins of Haughmond Abbey where he was seen to fall to his knees, praying for the White Lady to leave him in peace. Upon his return to the Manor, one of the maids told him a lady in white had visited and wished him to know she said goodbye. This was the final incident and soon after the vicar and his family moved from Pimley Manor.

One of the tenants who lived in Poplar flat in Pimley Manor was working in the front room when he and his partner felt the room temperature drop and they both saw, in the open doorway, a figure shaped by smoke in the male form that slowly vanished through the floorboards as the temperature warmed up again.

Raven Meadows

During the construction of the Darwin Shopping Centre, many of the construction workers on nightshift saw the ghost of a milkmaid with a yoke and pails walking around the site repeating, 'Weight and measure sold I ever, milk and water sold I never'. She is believed to be a milkmaid sentenced to death in the 1600 for selling watered-down milk. Throughout the short trial she maintained her innocence and vowed to eternally haunt the spot to prove her innocence.

Ye Old Bucks Head Inn, Shrewsbury

When the plague came to Shrewsbury for the second time it is believed to have been brought by a traveller who fell ill soon after arriving, and died before people knew what was wrong with him. Trying to find out who he was and what was wrong, nursing staff removed him from his room for burial. Several were bitten by fleas and fell ill themselves. Soon the plague was spreading out of control.

The sad part of this story is that a number of children from outlying areas already suffering the plague had been sent to the inn as a place of sanctuary. Within days they were either dead or dying in the place that was meant to be their salvation.

For many years, there has been seen a man washing his hands furiously, as if trying to rid himself of something. He wanders across the lawns of the youth hostel next door and at the windows of the private quarters of staff are seen children who appear happy, and then start to scratch at the windows screaming for help, their words never heard.

The site of the Battle of
Shrewsbury, 1403.

The Battle of Shrewsbury

In 1403 the Percy family, headed by the Duke of Norfolk, decided to rise against King Henry IV and marched towards London. Sir Henry Percy, known as Harry Hotspur, led his men from the north hoping to link up with the Lords and their men from Wales. The King had rallied his supporters and was rushing to head off the rebels. The King reached Shrewsbury first and was able to confront Harry Hotspur, who had gathered his men across the river. King Henry, with his son the Prince of Wales (later Henry V), rode into battle side by side. Across the fields from the town both sides faced each other on 21 July 1403. The King's men outnumbered Hotspur's six to one and had a superior number of longbows. This was the first time that longbows were used on English soil in warfare. There were so many arrows flying at the start of the battle that the sun was said to have been blocked out. Many thousands of men, women and children were killed within two hours. The remaining force on the side of Harry Hotspur turned and fled back north, leaving Harry and the majority of his men dead. The body of Harry Hotspur was taken to High Cross in Shrewsbury where the head was cut off and displayed on a pike, and the rest drawn and quartered as a warning to other rebels. The battlefield was covered four bodies deep in places and the stench was so great that the King and people of Shrewsbury raised funds to bury the bodies. Later the King founded a shrine to St Mary Magdalene, built as a church in 1547 to honour the fallen in one of the great battles of England.

Farming once again started when the fields were cleared of the thousands of arrows and the bodies. Within two years of the battle, groups of men, women and children were seen moving across fields before disappearing into the mists of time.

Berwick Wharf, Atcham

During the 1950s a small camp had been established on the disused Second World War airfield. Most were hard-working and willing to turn their hand to anything to make a living and keep the peace with the local communities. They were quickly accepted and some of the local youngsters would babysit for their new neighbours. On one such occasion, a young girl was babysitting for a man with three children. He had gone to the pub with a group from the camp and then said that he felt unwell and returned home. He was sweet on the young girl babysitting for him and thought she felt the same. He had been drinking and did not take kindly to her dismissing his advances with some distain. In a rage, he raped her before strangling her. Realising what he had done, he gathered up his victim, her clothes, shoes and handbag and disposed of all in a nearby airshaft for the old Shropshire canal. He continued on to the pub where he said he had seen some men walking toward the commune with sticks in an attempt to provide an alibi. When the group arrived home, two offered to take the babysitter home across the fields. When she could not be found they thought that she must have gone home early, leaving the children unattended. It was not until her parents and police visited that the community knew something was wrong.

The police searched the area but missed the airshaft and interviewed everyone at the camp. The killer managed to convince the police that he had too much to drink. He claimed to have been violently sick outside the pub, in the fields looking across to the camp, when he had seen the men and went back in to tell the others.

He must have thought he had got away with it as the days and weeks passed without her body being found. A local man was out walking his dog when he noticed a young woman sitting on the old brick canal airshaft, brushing her long hair. Being somewhat tipsy he thought nothing of it and went home to bed. The next morning he told his wife what he had seen and she just made the hand gesture of holding a drink. That night the *Shropshire Star* published a photograph of the murdered girl, but with shorter hair than the man had seen. He contacted the police, concerned that he might be wasting their time. They sent a policeman around to take down some more details. It was the fact that he had seen her with longer hair that was the clue. The photograph in the paper was a few years old and the girl had since let her hair grow in the style of the day. He took the search party to the airshaft and a policeman was lowered down on a rope. Just a few yards into the canal tunnel was what looked like a pile of old clothes. It was not until they got a boat in did they realise the bundle was the body of the murder victim. There was no DNA testing in those days, and all evidence of the murderer has been washed away in the canal water.

However, a few weeks later the murderer gave himself up, driven to admit his guilt by the sight of the girl standing at the end of his bed, dripping wet and beckoning him to follow her.

The Mytton & Mermaid, Atcham

The Mytton & Mermaid Hotel is a majestic building standing on the banks of the River Severn and is steeped in history. Built in the early 1700s, it was originally a coaching inn called the Talbot Arms, after the family name of the Earl of Shrewsbury. It was later rebuilt as an important posting house on the busy route from London to Ireland via Holyhead. In 1830 it was renamed the Berwick Arms after Lord Berwick of Attingham Park, and by the late 1860s it was a private home following the decline of coaching. Atcham House, as it became known, was purchased in 1932 by Sir Clough William-Ellis, the architect who created Portmeirion in North Wales. Atcham House became a high quality hotel for motorists and was renamed the Mytton & Mermaid, partly after the property's most famous owner, Mad Jack Mytton.

Mad Jack Mytton inherited a fortune at the age of twenty and for the next seventeen years, until his death on 30 September 1834, he lived life to excess. In his home he had 2,000 dogs,

Sundorne Castle before demolition.

sixty finely dressed cats and a pet bear, with whom he loved nothing more than drinking six bottles of port a day. He also liked to risk his life at least once every twenty-hour hours with such exploits as trying to jump the River Severn near the inn. He once set himself alight because he had hiccups. He had wild parties at the inn that lasted for days.

He died in a debtor's prison having wasted his great wealth. His body was released to his friends and they carried him to the inn where he lay in rest on the very table that had seen many a great party. They spent two days mourning before they buried him in the nearby churchyard.

To this day, on 30 September, Mad Jack Mytton returns to cause mischief and pinch the bottoms of the female staff. He has also been seen running along the ridge of the roof and bounding across the car park before leaping out into the river.

Old Canal, along Sundorne Road

Whilst out hunting in the late 1800s, a lady had her horse spooked by a child appearing from a bush as the hunt went past one of the entrances to the canal. The horse bolted, with the lady hanging on for dear life. As they approached a wall, the horse slipped and crashed into it head first. It broke its neck instantly and the lady slammed into a razor-wire fence on the other side of the wall that sliced through her throat and body. The others on the hunt could only look on as a doctor tried to stem the bleeding. She is still seen on the first day of the hunting season galloping on the field side of the road towards Haughmond Hill, holding on for dear life before both rider and horse are seen falling to the ground.

Rowton Castle

Rowton Castle is first mentioned in 1282 when it was destroyed by the Welsh, but it was apparently soon rebuilt, possibly by the Lovells, and around 1463 was acquired by the Lysters. Saxton's map of 1577 shows the castle and a park. During the Civil War it is reputed to have been besieged and destroyed by fire. The nineteenth-century castle seen today is now a delightful hotel with a friendly ghost that haunts Rooms 14 and 17. The ghost is a woman in her middle age dressed in a simple outfit, with dark hair tied in a bun. She appears a little stooped and those who have seen her feel she is in pain. She goes about her business checking the rooms day and night.

Pitchford Hall

Pitchford Hall is one of the best examples of a timber-framed building in Shropshire, and even has a miniature timber-framed tree house in the grounds. Queen Victoria was a frequent visitor to the hall… she enjoyed the ghost stories as much as the company.

Since 1473 the hall and estate have passed down a family line, with the last family owner being Mrs Oliver Colehurst, who inherited the estate from her step-father, Mr Robin Grant. He li uuld uuum in the hall smoking his favourite cigarillos imported from South America. A week after Robin Grant passed away the caretaker, Hugh Rennison, was putting dust sheets over the furniture when he smelt the whiff of the late owner's cigarillos.

To make room in the hall for the restoration work, the Rennisons moved into the North Lodge which had been modernised for them. One evening, Mr Rennison was late home due to unexpected guests arriving at the hall and was expecting his wife to moan about him being late. When he walked in his wife rushed to him and gave him a big hug. She was very pale and he asked if she had seen a ghost. She had. She went on to describe Robin Grant in a long black and white herringbone overcoat with a fur lining, smoking a cigarillo and looking at her as she was preparing the meal. She went on to say that there was a great feeling of wellbeing around him and she was not frightened.

Later, in 1991, Mr and Mrs Roberts moved in to the lodge after the Rennisons retired and took up working for Mrs Colehurst. Late one night, Mrs Roberts went to the bathroom and along the way met Robin standing by the entrance to the sitting room in his long coat with the glow of a cigarillo. Like Mrs Rennison, she felt no harm and was not frightened. The next day she told her husband about the man she had seen. He repeated the story to Mrs Colehurst who told him of her step-father, somewhat surprised by the detail his wife had seen because Robin Grant had died years before they joined the household.

The year before, Pitchford Hall opened to the public and many visitors caught the familiar whiff of cigarillo smoke. A heat engineer, Jeff Thomas, was staying with the family to work on the heating system and smelt a whiff of the smoke and saw the back of Robin going up the stairs in his big overcoat. The engineer saw other ghosts during his three week stay at the hall. The next he saw was a little old lady, wearing a dressing gown, who came out of the middle bathroom on the landing on the first floor and proceeded to totter to a room along the corridor. Whilst checking some pipes under the stairs he looked up to see a man dressed in black with chest plate armour, a large hat and black plume of feathers walking up the stairs – he thought the ghost was a cavalier. In the kitchen, when all the family were out shopping in Shrewsbury, he saw a tall woman in an apron walk through a locked door. The one place he did not like working was the library, as he felt that an angry ghost did not want him to be there. Two cleaners corroborated his story saying they felt that a very grumpy man did not want them in 'his' home and that they should 'beggar off'.

A psychic from Canada, Mr Russell Scharff, was taken around the hall by Mrs Colehurst and reported a number of ghosts, including Robin, whom he said was in his right frequency now. The psychic seemed to think that the worry of losing the hall from the family had driven him to an early grave whereas now, where he is, no matter who owns the hall, he will always be custodian of it. Mr Scharff told the family that a force that will not last forever protected the hall.

Mr Scharff walked to the kitchen where he felt the energy of a female who was quite tall and dedicated to the family. In a bedroom on the first floor he encountered two children playing around a large wooden travel case. This was the room where the young Princess Victoria slept with her mother, the Duchess of Kent, in 1832. Next door he felt the presence of a happy boy and a girl who were playing in and around the priest's hole. In the bathroom on the same floor he came across a pompous and overbearing character who had been very sceptical during his lifetime about the existence of ghosts, and so did not believe he was a ghost confined to one room.

In the bedroom between that bathroom and the next bedroom, he saw an image of a woman lying back on a chaise longue. He encountered the woman again in the next bathroom but this time she appeared to be fighting someone. He could not see who was trying to get her into the bath and felt she did not want to take a bath, as she was very frightened of the water.

Next door was a very elderly woman, asleep. In the nursery bathroom next door there was a woman lying in a heap on the floor who had died during childbirth. In the General's flat he felt the presence of a red-faced man in tweeds and breeches who seemed to be at peace with his lot. In the library, Mr Scharff saw a man sitting in a porter's chair – a servant – wearing blue breeches, a bright yellow coat with silver buttons and who had a huge smile. Before he left we walked up to the copse, an area of rough ground near the fishponds. Here, as he looked back at the hall, he became aware of the presence of a man who had committed suicide nearby. The owner had no idea who this could be, as she had no memory so just made a note of it. Later that day she went to the estate office to see the manager and asked if anyone had committed suicide near the ponds. His reply made her feel cold. The manager remembered that when he first came to the estate as an under manager, the old chap who was the estate manager told him a few ghost stories about the hall and one about the fishponds, or lakes as they were called. The gamekeeper, a Mr Whitterick, had been diagnosed with cancer just after his wife had passed away. A few days after he was told he had but a short time to live, he went up to the lake and, some say, just walked in singing 'Jerusalem'. He is seen walking into the lake during the summer months with his mouth moving but nothing heard.

A friend of the family who often stayed a night or two and who told fortunes for a living was asked by the owner if he thought the hall was haunted. He replied, 'My dear, the place is stuffed with them. They are all charming'.

He visited and the four of them, Mrs Colehurst, the Rector, Kath and Madge said the Lord's Prayer together in the library. It seemed to work for a while with the sightings and whiff of smoke stopping. All this was confirmed by one Barry Garside, who had rented the orangery and was a medium. He took a tour with Mrs Colehurst and described what he was picking up. He was emphatic that the grumpy female ghost in the hall was in fact one of Lady Lousa Jenkinson's sisters – either Selina or Catherine. When the 3rd Earl of Liverpool died, each daughter inherited a house and Lady Lousa inherited Pitchford, much to the annoyance of one of her sisters. He encountered a footman on the stairs, aimlessly standing awaiting orders. He was thoroughly fed up as his wife had been harassing him all day and now the master expected him to travel to London with him by coach on this very cold and wet night. In those days the footman travelled on the outside of the coach as a security guard against highway robbers. In an area known by the grandmother of the hall as flagellation corner, he picked up two young boys being punished by an older man, possibly their father who had caught them stealing from the kitchen. It was called that because it was here that the various riding whips were stored. In the attic, Mr Garside encountered two maids who were very excited to see the young master James Cotes ride down the drive returning from the Boer War in time for Christmas. In the General's flat he 'saw' a housekeeper wearily trudging the steps to her room – inwardly she was depressed as she was trying to come to terms with the loss of her brother.

Even the animals would notice ghosts moving through the rooms in which they lay. The ears of the cats and dogs would twitch and they would turn to watch someone walking across the room.

Condover Hall

Condover Hall has an interesting history as well as a sad haunting. The owner of the hall, Mr Kynvett, was a hard-working man and bestowed many a gift and allowance on his son. His son was ungrateful and anxious for his father to die in order for him to inherit the estate and so began to plot his murder. One night the son waited for the faithful butler to retire for the evening so that he could put his plan into action. As Mr Kynvett slept, his son silently crept up to his father's bed chamber and stabbed his father with a carving knife. His father rose to fend off his assailant and made it to the front door in a vain attempt to raise help. His injuries were so bad that he collapsed, covered in blood, and with the door open placed his bloody hand on the stone step as his life ebbed away. His last words were to curse his son to damnation.

To avert suspicion, the son pretended to arrive home late and blamed the butler, John Viam, for the murder. As there was no one else at Condover Hall at the time, the butler was sentenced to be hanged for the crime. Before he went to the gallows an innocent man, John Viam declared, 'Before Heaven, I am innocent, though my master's son swears me guilty and as I perish an innocent man may those who follow my murdered Lord be cursed'.

The second curse on the son was to be his final downfall. It is said that he went mad, claiming to see his father's face at the end of every corridor. His friends deserted him as they believed in John Viam's innocence and the son died in torment in the hall he had coveted. The blood stain on the front door step remained for many years; every time it was washed clean the handprint eerily returned. It was finally chiselled away.

Jiggers Bank

Jiggers Bank is a steep road down to Ironbridge from Shrewsbury and affords some great views of the countryside. There have been a number of sightings of a tall gentleman standing at the side of the road who strides into action if anyone has trouble getting up or down the hill. All those who have encountered him say they feel relaxed and happy that he should be helping them. One such sighting was by Miss Sears, who was having trouble with her Mini that broke down on the crown of the hill. She had some knowledge of engines as her brothers were keen mechanics. She tried all the tricks they had shown her, but to no avail. She got back in the Mini, bonnet still open, to wait for someone to pass. These were the days before mobile phones! As she sat in the car she saw a dark figure fiddling with the car, which suddenly fired into life. This was somewhat strange since the ignition was not switched on! She got out of the car to thank the stranger but he had vanished.

Long before that, a tinker with a wagon full of pots and pans was having trouble getting his cart up the steep hill as he had no horse or donkey to help him. As the cart started to roll backwards, with the tinker holding on to his source of living for dear life, a dark figure appeared behind the cart and helped push it to the top of the hill. When he had secured the cart to a tree, the tinker went to thank his helper, but no one was there.

A young delivery boy from an Ironbridge butchers was on his way to Leighton Hall one winter's day and so, with ice on the ground and no salting done, he braved the hill on his delivery bicycle. He was fine going up and safely made it to the hall, but halfway down his brakes broke away and he careered out of control speeding towards a cart coming up the hill. He closed his eyes fearing the collision. It never came. As soon as he closed his eyes he felt someone grab him off the bicycle and gently place him on the verge. The bicycle carried on, coming to rest under the large wheels of the cart. The drayman witnessing the event tried to pull the horses and cart out of the way of the speeding bicycle, but he too had closed his eyes and never got to see how the boy came to be safe on the verge. Despite the trouble he got into for causing damage to the delivery bicycle, the boy was only too thankful that the ghost of Jigger's Bank had saved him from possible death.

Rosehill House, Coalbrookdale

Rosehill House now forms part of the exciting and world-class living museum of Ironbridge Gorge. Built in 1730, it was once the home of Richard Ford, the clerk for the Coalbrookdale Company under Abraham Darby I. Ford went on to become the manager of the Coalbrookdale Iron Works. The house was later owned by the Darby family and has been restored by the Ironbridge Gorge Museum Trust to show how the house would have been in 1850.

The Darby family were Quakers and the furnishings simple. When they owned the house they had just four servants and managed the household in a frugal manner in keeping with their beliefs.

Perhaps the ghost of an old lady, seen in the garden looking out across the valley and inside in the kitchen knitting in a rocking chair, is one of the faithful servants who stayed with the generations of the Darby family at Rosehill House. Outside, a man in Victorian clothing is seen holding a tall hat, walking around the grounds and over at the rotunda some quarter of a mile away.

Coalbrookdale Warehouse

At the height of the Industrial Revolution this building was used as a warehouse for the Coalbrookdale Iron Works. It now houses the training centre, study library and exhibition rooms for the Ironbridge Gorge Museum Trust.

The first floor, near the stairwell, was the scene of a tragic accident. A young boy was helping move some large pieces of iron with his father using pulleys and rope. The unfortunate boy was crushed to death beneath a falling chunk of iron as the rope holding it broke. His helpless father stood by, unable to do anything but witness the death of his son. To this day, there is a feeling of cold on the stair and on some occasions the pitiful cries of a young lad in his last gasps of breath are heard.

On the road that runs alongside Coalbrookdale walks an old lady, believed to be the same lady who haunts Rosehill House; she sometimes stops and gazes back down the valley.

Buildwas Abbey

Buildwas Abbey began life in 1135 when the Bishop of Chester brought some Cistercian monks over from Normandy. It was built on the banks of the River Severn and it was the monks who built the first bridge to cross the river here. As testament to their skills the bridge stood the test of time until 1795 when it was washed away in the great floods. The bridge, which had four spans and measured 100ft across, was replaced by Thomas Telford with his first cast iron bridge. English Heritage owns the Abbey which is open to the public.

The Abbey was the scene of a foul deed. Sir Thomas Tong and other renegade monks entered the Abbey in 1342 and stabbed to death John Burnell, Abbot of Buildwas. The perpetrators were never caught as they fled abroad. The Black Abbot, as he is known, is seen walking the grounds searching for his killers. He also appears in the Abbey social club that was once part of the original building.

A recent suicide on the bridge has left a strange legacy. Many local people tried in vain to save a man who decided life was too much for him after his wife left him. Armed with a can of petrol he drove on to the bridge, poured the petrol over himself and the inside of the car and then struck a match. Fire engulfed the man and car in minutes. On quiet days locals have heard muffled screams and the smell of burning tyres.

The Power Station, Buildwas

Buildwas power station was built in 1965 with four cooling towers. The construction of these towers was not without tragedy. A man working high on the outer brick tower construction

Buldwas Abbey.

slipped, and with no safety harness fell to his death. The figure of a man has been seen at day and night, walking through the mists of the cooling water.

The station is still coal-fired, with a rail link to bring the coal that is now imported following the closure of the mine at Highley in 1969. The coal yard is cut in two by the old boundaries of the nearby Buildwas Abbey, home to the Black Abbot.

One worker was loading a great bucket of coal on to the conveyors that went to the furnaces, when he lifted the bucket he was shocked to notice a shadowy figure standing where he had just taken coal. He pointed the tractor's spotlight on the area. No one was there. As the light moved from the area, the figure reappeared. Puzzled, he got down from the cab to warn the person to get out of the way, as this is a dangerous area to be walking. As he approached the figure, he saw that the person was dressed as a monk, who then faded away right in front of his very eyes. He broke all the speed records as he got back in the cab and drove off down the road to the safety of the staff room where it took his supervisor an hour and more to get him back to work.

The Old Warehouse

This is a fine example of Gothic revival architecture with its turrets and battlements. The main purpose of the building was loading and unloading the Severn trows travelling up and down the river from Bristol. It is now the river museum for the Ironbridge Gorge Museum Trust.

In front of the building is a slipway with tracks used to guide the wagons that travelled between the trows and the warehouse. During the early morning rush, when safety was but a second thought, children were used as brakemen, putting blocks under the wagon to stop them rolling too fast down the incline to the waiting trows. A young lad who had been working through the night to get loads off a number of trows was sleepy and did not hear the warning cry from his gang master. He struggled to pull his block from under the wagon he was braking. A runaway wagon, full of off-loaded goods, hit the lad and swept him to his death, crushed between the wagon and the sailing barge. The tragic little figure of the lad is seen pulling at his invisible block before vanishing.

The Old Warehouse.

The Iron Bridge

This is the first bridge in the world made of iron, and forms the centre of the World Heritage Site. It is made using the same design techniques as a wooden bridge, using iron 'pegs' to hold the structure together. Below the bridge flows the River Severn towards Bristol and the sea.

In the dead of night, silently shrouded in a mist, a boat similar in shape and size to a Severn trow glides slowly down the river towards Jackfield, where it is also seen tied up and unloading its secret cargo. At the helm stands a tall figure with a hood covering his features. Upon the deck and in the hold is the gruesome cargo of bodies. During the fifteenth and sixteenth centuries, plague bodies were collected and buried in lime-lined pits to contain the disease. Some people who had developed immunity to the plague were used to help move the bodies either to a pyre or to a lime-lined pit.

The Tontine Hotel

This family-run hotel opposite the Iron Bridge has a restless ghost. 'Fred', as he is nicknamed, is thought to be the ghost of one of the last men to be hanged in Shropshire, after he murdered Mrs Janet Edge, licensee of the Queen's Head Inn, Ketley. He had robbed the landlady before murdering her, then fled to the Tontine Hotel. He managed to stay in Room 5 for a few days before he was arrested. He was executed on 4 January at 8 a.m. in 1951 in the stone execution shed at the rear of Shrewsbury Prison.

Since then people staying in Room 5 have felt that someone was watching them, lights turn on and off and there is a strange smell of cheap aftershave in the room and on the stairway. Taps in the room turn on and off and clocks run backwards at 8 a.m.

The Iron Birdge, with the Tontine Hotel behind.

Benthall Edge

During the Victorian period a manager was carrying wages for his workers at the lime works on Benthall Edge. He normally had someone with him when he carried the money back to the quarry but his colleague who had travelled with him to collect the wages claimed to have suddenly been taken ill and stayed at Ironbridge. Leaving Ironbridge on his own, the manager made his way through the woods to the lime quarry. He never made it to the quarry office as the very colleague he had left in Ironbridge and an accomplice set upon him. They relieved him of the wages with force and then tied and gagged him, before throwing him mercilessly down an old pit shaft. They then placed a heavy stone over the top. His shouts went unheard due to the noise from the surrounding lime works. After some hours of searching the man was found crushed to death by the large slab of stone. In his efforts to get out of his tomb he had dislodged the stone. It was only on his deathbed years later that one of the robbers confessed to the entombment. He regretted the death of the manager who had given him a job when he most wanted it. When walking along the edge you may hear the shouts of the man from his tomb that echo along the edge.

Nearby is the pool on Benthall Edge, just above the power station. On certain days the pool turns a deep red, as if boiling with blood. The story is that this is the blood of a young woman who was savagely raped and murdered by workers from the limestone works. She had been walking to Ironbridge from the small keeper's cottage to meet her fiancée on a warm summer day. Her fiancée began to worry when she did not arrive at the Tontine and went up along the ridge to find her. Had he not been seen at the Tontine, he may well have been the main suspect because he was the first to see his fiancée lying face down in the pool, clothes ripped and blood all over her face, hands and legs. The bedraggled, distressed figure is seen near the pool gazing down into the waters of the pool that turns from shimmering blue to deep red.

Benthall Pool.

The Boat Inn, Jackfield

The Devil was said to have visited the Boat Inn just before Christmas to play cards with unsuspecting locals on a Sunday. It was only when a card dropped on the floor and one of the party leant down to pick it up that he noticed the hoofed feet of their new companion. No sooner had the Devil realised his identity has been unmasked than a great gust of wind blew through the door, throwing the men, table and chairs to the wall. The Devil vanished into the night, leaving behind the souls he had been playing cards to win. Legend has it that to play cards on a Sunday would summon the Devil who could steal your soul away.

More recently, the landlady awoke to see a young lady standing at the side of her bed, pointing and beckoning her to go downstairs. Her husband was away that night so she was reluctant to leave her bed and accompany the figure. When she plucked up enough courage to go downstairs, she found that the window the young girl was pointing to had been forced open. No one had gained access and when she looked back at the girl, she had vanished.

Ferry Road, Jackfield

During the winter months the River Severn rises and becomes treacherous. It was at such a time that young twins were playing on the spoil heaps from the Craven-Dunhill tile works. The recent heavy rain had made the spoil heap unstable and it collapsed as the twins played, plunging them into the river. They drowned as they were swept down river, their bodies snared in a tree that had been washed downstream and caught under the footbridge a few yards on. Following an exhaustive search they were spotted, and their tiny bodies recovered from the river, still holding hands. They were taken to the first cottage on Ferry Road. To this day, the children are seen splashing in the river in front of the bridge and heard crying for their mother along the small road and in the garden of the first house in the terrace along Ferry Road.

St Michael's Church, Madeley

St Michael's Church is an impressive building, towering above Madeley, and is home to a wonderful array of cast iron grave markers. The graveyard was once a short cut to the nearby mines. One morning, at about 7 a.m., a coal miner was walking to work when he noticed a figure moving about the graves through the light mist. As he moved closer he saw it was an old woman placing flowers on a grave and making it tidy. He stumbled, and lost sight of the old woman for a few seconds. He looked for her but she had vanished. He walked to the site of the grave he had seen to find it overgrown and the stone worn away, with no sign of the fresh flowers. Looking around he could see there was no way out of this part of the graveyard, just a high hedge and deep ditch beyond. Who was she and who was the person buried there?

Ferry Road, Jackfield.

Madeley Court House

Madeley Court is recorded in *The Domesday Book* of William the Conqueror, but it is known that a building had been on the site since the Saxon Period. In the eighth century, St Milburga is reputed to have bought the Madeley estate from Sigward, a follower of King Ethelbald of Mercia. The last Prior of Madeley was John Bayley; he surrendered the priory and its estates to the commissioners of Henry VIII in 1540.

Madeley is the crucible of the industrial revolution. The High Street and Court Street are now part of the Ironbridge Gorge World Heritage Industrial Site.

In 1705 Comberford Brooke sold the property to Matthias Astley, who leased the property to the first Abraham Darby, who died there in 1717. The surrounding area was mined for the coal vital to the industrial revolution. The developments at Ironbridge and Coalbrookdale have left a mound-riddled landscape around three sides of the building. It had fallen into ruin before the newly formed Telford Development Corporation took it over and started to consolidate the buildings which date from the thirteenth century, with sixteenth and seventeenth-century additions including the gatehouse. This fine Elizabethan manor house is now a luxury hotel befitting its rich history, and also has many strange goings on.

At one time there was a row of miner's cottages in the hollow, now a football pitch. Long-past inhabitants of the cottages still return to stoke up their home fires. Often people walking along the track see smoke rising from invisible chimneys. One of the strangest sights is that of a partial front door that opens, and the face of a woman appears, smiles, and then disappears.

In the manor house itself there have been seen a number of monks who not only walk through the walls but are also known to sit on the tie-beams of the Great Hall. There is a rumour that a tunnel ran from here, once a monastery, to the nearby windmill and then a local inn.

A witch roamed the area catching children and selling their souls to the Devil for pieces of silver. She would disguise herself as a large hare and tempt children to stroke her before grabbing them and taking them off to her hovel. The locals heard of the story of the large hare

Madeley Court House.

and decided to chase and capture it. They cornered it a few times, wounding it on the face and side. It ran so hard that all four paw pads were bleeding profusely. They tracked the blood stains to a small hovel and observed the pad prints changing shape to human footprints that led to the front door. Inside they found the witch in her human form bleeding from hands, face, feet and side. The mob dragged her to the side of a clearing and burnt her alive. Before their eyes she changed into her animal form before vanishing into the flames.

The Old Windmill

The Silkin Way footpath is a well-used route from Madeley to Brookside, and runs close to the old windmill. Built in 1702, it last worked as a mill in 1840. A young man, having been to see his girlfriend at Brookside, was walking home when he noticed the windmill sails working, accompanied by the groaning noise of a working mill. This was strange since the mill was derelict. Either side of the mill he described seeing two figures, half-man, and half goat, knocking the sails around. He did not go any further, turned back and ran to his girlfriend's home at Brookside.

Another strange incident occurred nearby. While walking her dog over an old pit mound, the walker suddenly became confused and was rendered deaf. She could hear no sound, although she could see people playing football in the field below and cars driving by in the distance. Putting her hands to her ears she suddenly became aware of a deep black hole opening a few feet in front of her and she could see her dog standing at the other side barking a warning at her. It turned out to be an old airshaft of one of the old coal mines in the area. Almost as suddenly as it went, her hearing returned.

Woodside, Coalbrookdale

A young son of the house recently saw a figure of a woman brushing her hair, as if in a mirror, at the bottom of his bed. When he told his mother, she was very upset. Her son's room had been her sister's room before he was born. She had been killed in a road accident a few miles away, and she used to have a vanity unit where the end of her son's bed was. Three days later the son then said he had seen an older woman walking up and down in front of the window, sometimes stopping to look out. She showed him photographs of her late mother and her son confirmed the older woman he had seen and described was the same as the lady in the photograph. Her son was moved out of the room, which was made into a small sitting room and the sightings stopped. Yet every now and then, the scent of her mother and sister would linger in that room.

Chockleys Meadow, Leegomery, Telford

In October 1985, the Ralphs family moved into their new home, rented from the Telford Development Corporation. All was well; they had a great Christmas and looked forward to the New Year in their new home. However, all was not well with the house. Mrs Ralphs started to see a tall figure dressed in black walk through her kitchen wall. Then the daughter, Julie, also saw the figure, but this time on the landing outside the bathroom. Strange things began to happen, like lights switching themselves on and off, loud knocking noises from the ground that sounded like a train running under the house and ever more sightings. The family were so upset by the haunting that they ended up living in one room. The housing officers called but did not experience anything unusual, although they all remarked how cold the house felt even with the heating on. The family were eventually moved to another address and the hauntings ceased.

Hollinswood, Telford

This is another modern house, part of a housing estate built on fields, which has a haunting that cannot be explained. The teenage daughter of the house was fast asleep when she awoke to a gentle rocking of her bed. Thinking it was a school day, she muttered something to the person she took to be her mother and rolled over. The shaking continued but with much more force. The girl was not amused and turned to tell her mum to stop. She came face to face with a tall, older woman who was at the side of her bed. She smiled at her and asked who she was. There was no reply and the woman walked out of the bedroom. It was an early Saturday morning and the girl fell back to sleep. She was not unduly worried by the appearance of the old woman, as she had been meeting lots of her mother's relations and just assumed this was another one of them. When she finally got up and asked who the annoying woman was, her parents looked puzzled. No one had been in the house at all except them and her brother who had gone out with his friends. The girl went cold as she realised it must have been a ghost. For weeks she slept with a light on. As soon as she was brave enough to sleep in the dark, the visitations began again, this time with real anger. The girl screamed and the figure vanished – never to be seen again.

Brookside Play Area, Telford

One summer holiday, some boys were playing on the new swings and climbing frames when they saw a man with a Jack Russell dog walking along the side of the hedge. He suddenly looked up and shouted to them to 'Get off my land!' and he waved his fist They ran over towards the man, who disappeared behind a large oak tree. Running behind it, the boys could not find the man or his dog. He had vanished into thin air. They were even more perplexed when he reappeared behind them shouting, 'Get off my land!' before vanishing in front of their very eyes. Was he the old farmer who lived at the farm before it was demolished to make way for the new housing estate?

The Ketley Tiger, Raymond Avenue

The development of Ketley into Telford New Town has meant much has changed, yet effort has been made to retain some of the Shropshire characteristics amongst the new housing estates and shops. Sadly, one place that has disappeared is the green on which May fairs were celebrated. It was also the scene of great excitement when the circus came to town, drawing visitors from miles around, from villages and surrounding parishes and even further afield. The idea of seeing real lions and tigers was too good an opportunity to miss.

During a trip from a Donnington school, three young boys managed to escape their strict form mistress and hid amongst the costumes. An hour later, when staff were taking lunch with the rest of the school parties, the three boys went to the tiger cage and started to poke it with a broom they found propped up by the cage. For a while the tiger just lay there and took the poking. Then it got up and started to pad around its cage. The boys started to shout at the tiger, angering it more when suddenly it pounced at them, grazing the arm of one of the boys . In a second angry leap, the tiger smashed into the iron bars of the cage and broke its neck on impact. The boys ran away, leaving the keeper to come across his hapless tiger. The green is now a road and traffic island on which some motorists have seen a tiger padding around an invisible cage before leaping and vanishing. During 1978, stories of big cat sightings scared the local residents and some, not familiar with the circus story, panicked when reports of a tiger being seen on the traffic island were rumoured.

Ketley Brook

Two men were out poaching for rabbits when they had to cross two fields and a ditch. As they were laying nets, one of them spotted what looked like a police officer in a tall hat coming

The Ketley Tiger.

towards them. They panicked and both jumped over a barbed wire fence, on which one of them cut his leg. The figure was still walking towards them so they decided that the best thing to do was ask the time to put the police officer off the trail. They watched the figure getting closer – and then vanish. Word has it that they were quicker out of the field than their dogs!

Apley Pool

On 9 February 1883, the head of a young girl was found stuffed into a sack on the shore of Apley Pool, a discovery that brought to light one of the most horrific murders of the nineteenth century.

Polly Mayas lived in the small village of Kynnersley with her father, Richard, and wicked stepmother, Elizabeth, and three of Elizabeth's children. Polly was not wanted by Elizabeth and was often seen by her neighbours neglected and starving for both food and affection. Her father worked long hours to keep the family fed, so often Polly was in bed when he came in from work and so he did not notice his daughter's decline at the hands of his new wife. Elizabeth frequently beat Polly, with the neighbours desperately stepping in to stop her. During the next beating, Polly was knocked out cold. Polly later died from a fractured skull, so in a panic Elizabeth cut up the body and tried to burn it. When that did not work, she put the body parts into sacks and gave them to her husband to dump as kitchen waste. The neighbours feared the worst when Polly vanished and they were told by Elizabeth that Polly had gone to an institution in Shrewsbury where she would be taught a trade as a seamstress.

Once the facts about Polly's murder came to light, the cottage was ransacked by an angry mob and all of Elizabeth's clothes burnt in the street. Extra police officers were drafted in to stop Wellington police station from being overrun, the police feared that Elizabeth and her husband would be lynched, such was the outrage of the local people. When the police tried to drive a horse-drawn carriage through the crowds with the couple inside, the mob nearly turned the carriage over and mounted police had to clear the way.

Because of the high level of outrage, the two were committed for trial at Stafford where Mr Justice Stephens heard the case on 26 April 1883. Polly's father was acquitted of murder but given eighteen months hard labour for being an accessory after the fact. Elizabeth was said to have mental problems and so was given twenty years for manslaughter. She died within six years of her imprisonment.

What is strange is how the head was first found. Two poachers out along the banks of Apley Pool saw a young girl paddling in the shallows. As they approached her, their dogs started to bark at a sack floating in reeds by the girl. Distracted, they took their eyes off her for a second to see what was exciting the dogs. Imagine the shock of opening the sack to see the partly-burnt head of the girl looking up at them from the bottom of the sack!

Swinbatch Farm

Before a young family of eight moved into the farmhouse at Swinbatch, the previous tenant had been taken ill in the fields and returned to the front sitting room where he later died. The room was used by the new family as a snooker room. It was always a cold room, even with the large wood burner fully stoked and fired.

The first indications of a haunting were seen by the eldest daughter. Hearing footsteps outside her ground floor bedroom window, she went to investigate. It was a partly moonlit night and visibility was good. She saw the figure of an old man bent up in agony. He turned the corner and disappeared from view. Other members of the family and visitors to the house have seen him and heard him open the latch door at the bottom of the stairs, walk slowly up the stairs and onto the landing where the footsteps stop. He is also seen in the kitchen, three of the downstairs rooms and in the farmyard.

His neighbour lived in a small cottage on the edge of the valley running down to the River Severn, near a narrow gauge rail track that took coal and ironstone from the mines above Swinbatch Farm. The cottage is a ruin now and difficult to find. Archaeologists from the Ironbridge Gorge Museum Trust were surveying the old track when one of the team pointed out a cottage on the other side of the valley that did not appear on their plans. It had roses in the garden, smoke rising from the chimney and a young woman tending a few chickens outside. Intrigued, the party of five made their way across the valley to investigate. In the bottom of the valley they lost sight of the cottage but carried on up the other side. When they finally reached the spot, all they found was a derelict ruin, a few broken cups and plates on the floor and no sign of life whatsoever.

Linley Hall, Near Broseley

In 1860 the ghost of a monk was seen in a dream by a young lady staying at the hall. She was a guest of the family and due to marry a local gentleman, Mr Pierson-Gordon. She went to bed but heard knockings coming from the fireplace, so she got up and knocked back in the sequence she had heard. After a short time the knocking stopped and she went back to bed. As she slept, she saw in her dreams a monk walking towards her, telling her she must open the left-hand side of the chimney as there was something there he needed her to find and show the world. She took no notice of the dream until she had the same dream the following night. She recounted her dream to the lady of the house, Mrs Lowndes, who in turn told her husband. He was somewhat sceptical but arranged for one of the estate staff to knock a hole in the wall. Hidden in an alcove in the wall, large enough to accommodate a man, they found a miniature portrait of a monk, a robe and a cross carved crudely in wood. The items were moved to the study and the hole bricked up. The ghostly knockings immediately stopped, but a monk is still seen in the grounds.

Dawley Parish Church

In the late 1800s a young woman, Martha, who was in service to the local squire of Dawley found she was pregnant and upon telling the squire her news was thrown out of his household with nowhere to go. Not having a husband to support her and her unborn child, she took the only option she saw – to commit suicide. She went to the parish church and spent some time inside contemplating suicide before the verger asked her to leave, as they did not allow parishioners to stay in the church overnight. She walked in to the graveyard and, using a razor,

The monk of Linley Hall.

she was seen to cut her own throat. The verger rushed to her aid but she jumped over the low graveyard wall, right into the path of a man returning from work. He screamed and ran off; she must have looked like a demon with blood all over her face, hands and dress. She picked herself up and weakly made for the well that was in the field opposite the church. Perhaps the cut was not too deep and she had gone to wash the blood off... we will never know. The verger, being elderly, could not jump the wall and went directly to the vicarage to summon help. When help arrived no sign of Martha could be found – until the light from one of their oil lamps shone on her body floating face down in the well. Because she had taken her own life, she was buried outside the church grounds, as was the custom – some believe in the meadow. To this day the blood-covered spectre of Martha jumps over the wall and heads off in the direction of the well where she drowned. When you are walking along the footpath of Dawley Parish Church at night, say a prayer and look out for Martha.

Willey Hall and Tom Moody

Tom Moody was spotted by Lord Forrester of Willey Hall as he raced a wild horse across one of his fields. He summoned Tom to the hall and offered him a job in the stables. Tom was only too pleased to accept. Someone once said of Tom, 'He was like a winged Mercury, making light both of stone walls and five-feet six inch gates. He was a regular centaur, for he and his horse seemed as one'. Tom enjoyed the thrill of the chase and soon became the whipper-in for the hunt, keeping the hounds on the scent of the fox. Tom was terrified of being buried alive and of suffering the same sleeping sickness that took the gentleman in Shrewsbury who was buried alive in St Julian's Church. He had a feeling that the time for his death was getting close and told his master, Lord Forrester, his final wishes:

When I am dead I wish to be buried at Barrow, under the yew tree, in the churchyard there, and to be carried to the grave by six earth stoppers; my old horse, with my whip, boots, spurs and cap slung on each side of the saddle, and the brush of the last fox when I was up at the death, at the side of the forelock, and two couples of old hounds to follow me to the grave as mourners. When I am laid in the grave let three halloos be given over me; and then, if I don't lift my head, you may fairly conclude that Tom Moody's dead.

It was not long afterwards that Tom died and Lord Forrester did exactly as Tom had requested. On his grave is the simple inscription:

Tom Moody

Buried Nov 19th

1796

In a painting of Tom at his peak, a second Tom in the form of a ghost was added. Tom Moody lives on in poems, songs, stories and paintings about the famous Shropshire lad. His ghost appears around the Willey Hall with his trusted hound by his side and is said to appear in the hall if one of the Forrester family is about to join him.

Hall Close Farm, Alveley

Hall Close Farm is a delightful Shropshire timber-framed house with a carved human head on the timber of the porch. It is three storeys high with one room that has a window to the outside but has no access from inside. The story is that it is was part of an extension that was never completed after the owner went into gambling debt and committed suicide in the room. Looking in from

Tom Moody at Willey Hall.

the outside, the walls are still wattle but without daub and there are no floorboards. Sometimes the face of a man appears in the window for a short while before disappearing from view.

On Christmas morning 1983, Sheila Jones woke to see an old man and woman standing at the bottom of her bed. The old woman repeatedly called for Dolly. Sheila woke her sister, Delia, who could not see or hear the couple. It was not until some years later that an old photograph album was found and inside were photographs of the old couple Sheila had seen. It was her grandparents, who had died before Sheila was born. A while later in the same bedroom, Delia woke to see a grey-haired gentleman at a writing desk using a quill. He looked around at her and turned back and continued to write. She pulled her bedding over her head and fell asleep. The girls brother awoke to see a woman crying, 'Come with me, come with me, my husband is being hanged' as she held a knife in one hand and a length of rope in the other.

There is a room where sometimes guests are accommodated, only for them to wake in the middle of the night and run downstairs to the kitchen where they spend the rest of the night. They do not see anything, but have a real sense of doom that makes them feel physically sick.

There is also an old woman who seems to keep an eye on the children for one night. Paul, one of the children, had been out late and his mother had put his meal in the range to stay warm. As he sat down to eat at about two o'clock in the morning, he noticed the latch lift and the door to the kitchen open. A woman in her sixties or seventies stood in the doorway and smiled at him. She turned and closed the door behind her. Paul was so taken by her that he followed her down the corridor and saw her climb the stairs towards the ghost room. He decided to go back down to the kitchen to finish off his meal, but decided not to sleep upstairs!

Lower Edgebold Farm, Handwood

The owner of a small estate he ran from his farmhouse, Mr Oakley was out collecting the rent from his tenants when he was set upon by some local thugs who had been drinking in Handwood. They pulled him from his cart and beat him, stealing the rent that amounted to just 7s. They left him for dead at the side of a track, thinking no more about it as they went to the pub. Mr Oakley's horse and cart returned to the farm and his housekeeper raised the alarm. Farm workers turned out to search for Mr Oakley, who was found slumped in a hedge, close to death. He was taken home but died before the doctor arrived. No one was charged for the crime, although locals had an idea of who the culprits were and ran them out of the village. A week after the funeral Mr Oakley was seen walking towards the village and his face appeared in the window of his home, much to the distress of his housekeeper.

three

SOUTH SHROPSHIRE

The Old Chemist Shop, Much Wenlock

The chemist shop has had a few tragedies and more than its fair share of suicides. Just after the building was completed the wife of the owner was found hanging by her dress on the landing outside her bedroom. She is said to constantly cry out for the help of her husband, who never makes it to save her. In the 1930s, a chemist committed suicide by drinking gin and arsenic after he made a mistake in a prescription for a young child that died as a result. During the refurbishment of the building in 1982, the workmen had removed much of the timber flooring from the upper levels. They were taken aback when they heard distinct footsteps on non-existent wooden floors upstairs. Climbing the stairs to see what was going on, one younger member of the team looked around the upper floors but could find nothing to account for the noise. He came downstairs to tell his colleagues and as he finished his words there was a mighty bang from upstairs and a large metal pole came crashing down the stairs. Since the work was completed there have been other strange happenings, more footsteps heard, and paintings and objects pulled off the walls and placed on the floor at night.

The George & Dragon

Known for the excellent atmosphere, food and beer, the George & Dragon has a more sinister side to its history. Many years ago, a cruel landlord beat not only his staff, but family and dogs, and kept a large black dog in the cellar to guard the ale he brewed on site. The poor animal was beaten if it tried to get out into the fresh air and thrown back down the stone stairs to the cellar floor. The only food and water he had was taken to him by a young maid who the landlord had bought off her parents for a few shillings. She worked hard, from daybreak to nightfall, and sometimes slipped into the cellar to sleep alongside the dog for warmth. Eventually the dog passed away and broke the heart of the maid who can still be heard weeping in the cellar.

The Guildhall, Much Wenlock.

The black dog wanders the cellar and the bar area, walking around under the tables looking for the maid and anyone who will make a fuss of him. A word of warning though – if you are privileged to see the black dog, do not be surprised if you go to stroke him and all you feel is cold air.

The Antique Shop, High Street, Much Wenlock

During the restoration of an antique shop in the High Street in 1984, the articulated skeleton of an adult male was discovered underneath a stud wall. As the archaeologists excavated more of the site, they unearthed the remains of two young ladies adjacent to the male. It is thought they may be Saxon or Roman civilians who lived in the town. For many years, local residents have seen a small group of people, heads down, shuffling around the yard and in the nearby passage.

Just around the corner from the antique shop is Renolds House; it has a distinctive appearance with its fine timber-frame with a mid-floor balcony. Built in 1682, it has had a chequered history, including periods of neglect. During one such derelict phase the faces of young children appeared at the leaded windows and on the balcony, playing with a spinning top, accompanied by shrill laughter. The children are always seen wearing their Sunday best and waving happily through the windows.

Bridgnorth Castle

Bridgnorth Castle looks out over the Severn valley and towards the Midlands. The ruin of the castle, a once-splendid building blown up during the Civil War for being a Royalist stronghold, has a number of ghosts. One of the ghosts may be the same one that appears at the Governor's house in nearby East Castle Street, built in 1633 as a residence of the castle governor.

Bridgnorth Castle ruins.

A ghost rider is heard fast-approaching the keep on a cobbled surface. The rider dismounts and is heard running in the direction of the inner keep. No one has seen the phantom, but many have heard it on winter nights. The ghost rider is believed to be the Royalist despatch rider who was killed on his way to tell his mother to escape Bridgnorth as the Parliamentarians were *en route* to attack the town. The horse is said to arrive at the door, which is pushed open and booted footfall is heard running upstairs to what was Lady Benthall's bedchamber. Some accounts of the ghost suggest that it sounded like the horse went up the stairs too!

Perhaps the town's best ghost story is one witnessed on a number of occasions by two police officers on night duty. One night when the air was mild, they noticed a young woman dressed in a long hooded cloak and laced boots.

Nigel Evans was one of the police officers to see the woman. He had arranged to meet up with a colleague at 1.45 a.m. to have a chat and a cigarette. The first night they saw the woman in black, they thought nothing of it as they walked down the Cartway to low town. She was in her thirties; tall, slim and wearing a long cape, like fancy dress. The second night, he met his colleague again and the woman appeared just before 2 a.m. PC Evans asked if she was alright and she replied, 'Yes thank you', before vanishing down Cartway. They were a little worried that she was out on her own, so the next night stood at the top of Cartway and waited for her to appear. Sure enough, at just before 2 a.m. she appeared, but as she turned into Cartway she disappeared. Both were sure that she must have dived into a doorway, so walked down the Cartway checking every door but found no sign of her. The next night they decided to stand at the top of the Cartway to watch what happened to her. Just before 2 a.m. the other officer was called away to an incident along the high street. PC Evans waited and the woman appeared, turned, went down the Cartway, turned and walked straight through a wall. One explanation for her appearance is that a young woman had been betrayed by her lover and committed suicide. After that they did not see her again and soon after, PC Evans was posted to Broseley.

Mr Evans' account is on record and there is evidence that a number of suicides have taken place in and around Cartway over the years. However a local reporter, Brian Hill, decided to stake out the Cartway. On his first night watch, he was amazed to see a woman dressed in a black cloak walking towards him. He also noticed that the woman had trouble keeping still – she appeared to hover. He asked her name and recognised it as someone living in the town. He went back many times to see if he could see the woman in black again and on three occasions, just after 2 a.m., she would appear. He now had a good idea of who the living woman was and during daylight hours he walked past her home and saw the same woman he had met and seen vanishing through a wall in Cartway. There is a school of thought that the mind has the power to project itself in a physical form, as with the young woman seen outside the Feathers Hotel in Ludlow.

The Magpie House (now Bassa Villa)

The restaurant once known as the Magpie House, now the Bassa Villa, is haunted by another lady in black. The story behind the haunting is a tragedy. Two children, brother and sister Charlotte and William, were left at home playing hide and seek. They found the cellar door open and decided to explore. The children were running around the cellar but soon tired and decided to go back upstairs and wait for their mother who had popped out to the shops. The cellar door was jammed and they could not open it. Meanwhile, the River Severn had burst its banks and started to flood the cellar. The children drowned in the freezing cold water and were discovered by their mother many hours later after a frantic search. The children have not been seen, but there are two marble busts in memory of them outside the building on the terrace. They have been heard by many people, including Mrs Cole, a previous owner, who has seen the mother walk through her wardrobe door. One Christmas Eve the lady dressed in black entered her bedroom, sobbing into a white handkerchief, as she went and lay down on the bed besides Mrs Cole. Mrs Cole felt no fear, just the overwhelming grief of the mother.

The Magpie House.

Abanazer's Cottage

Abanazer's Cottage is in Ebenezer Row, Bridgnorth. Mr John Furness has owned the property since 1985. The cottage has been occupied continuously since it was built in 1810. The occupant before Mr Furness was a little old man who lived alone and would not open the door to anyone. Mr Furness spent the first year working on the cottage, making it habitable. He would stay late at night and on two occasions, he passed the previous owner, the little old man, on the stairs and walked straight through him. Since living in the cottage, he has felt the presence of the old man many times. The ghost, nicknamed Charlie, appears to live in the attic and shuffles around at night. Mr Furness says that Charlie is no trouble and his theory is that the old man felt so safe in the cottage that upon his death, he was reluctant to leave.

Old Mo

Very little is known of the history of the Bridgnorth Franciscan Friary, not even the exact date of its foundation. It must have been founded after 1224 when the Franciscans first came to England, but before 1244 when Henry III ordered payment of 40s to the Friars Minor of Bridgnorth towards the building of their church. There is no reliable record of the name of the founder, claimed by later friars to be Ralph le Strange.

Bridgnorth Friary was typical in its position on the outskirts of one of the poorer quarters of the town, on a confined strip of land on the west bank of the Severn to the north of the bridge.

The Friary was surrendered on 5 August 1538. The King's Commissioner described it as the poorest house he had seen, with 'all the houses at fallyng downe'. By 1860 nothing remained of the Friary.

Old Mo, a monk at the Friary, was known to drink and mix with women of the night. Despite warnings from fellow monks, he carried on his unholy ways until the brethren could take no more. One night, as he returned from his night out he was confronted by a group of monks who tried to reason with him, but to no avail. The situation turned violent. Old Mo was bludgeoned and then poisoned; no one knows where his body was disposed of – it may have been in the river or buried in the grounds. What is known is that Old Mo continues to haunt the district.

The Bridgnorth carpet factory was built on the site of the Friary and was itself demolished in the late 1980s and early 1990s to make way for new housing on the riverside. Part of the site was excavated by a team of archaeologists. Human remains were found, along with part of the original Friary building. Some of the exposed buildings were saved. During the Second World War the factory was commandeered to build components for aero engines. During this period, Mr Bert James was on duty one night when he saw the spirit of a man dressed in a grey habit tied at the waist by a rope cord. Was this Old Mo?

Mr Ceil Rushton had a similar encounter with Old Mo one evening in 1949 while walking his dog. When passing an entrance surrounded by railings which led underneath the factory, his dog let out a spine-chilling howl and ran off into the night. Looking around

Mr Rushton saw a figure in a long purple robe glide from the factory and down towards the river.

Over the years many people claim to have laid eyes on Old Mo. One eyewitness account from a carpet factory employee said:

> It was in November about 6.30, I was in the stock room, I looked up, I see him sort of hovering towards me, a tall chap dressed in a monks coat with the hood up, I didn't see his face, but I didn't hang round to say me hellos, I was off on me heels, I went up the pub and had a few Brown Ales.

After the factory closed the spirits remained at rest, until a modern housing development disrupted the peace. Old Mo is back to his wandering!

Acton Arms

The Acton Arms is thought to be one of the most frequently haunted inns in the country. Little is known of the ghost except that he is the figure of a monk and fits the description of Old Mo, whose story was told in the previous account. Old Mo was known to have frequented local inns in the sixteenth century.

The monk is most often seen upstairs appearing as a 'white form' and only vaguely in the shape of a man. His figure has been seen in an upstairs corridor moving from room to room. His appearances are daily and on occasions he has been seen more than once on the same day. He has often been seen in one of the bedrooms, standing quietly in the corner watching out of a window.

No. 11 High Street, Bridgnorth

No. 11 High Street was built in the early 1700s, and was formerly a sweet shop with living quarters on the first floor. The only history of the premises reports a possible suicide on the first floor, but the date of such an event cannot be verified.

The first records talk of a cleaning lady who used to look after the first floor. She became so unsettled that she asked a friend to help her. When her friend came with her she brought her dog. The dog became so anxious on entering the building that it would not follow her up the stairs.

The second event relates to two decorators who were employed to decorate the rooms on the first floor at night. One of the decorators fell asleep on the settee in the living room and was suddenly awoken by what he thought was his friend shaking him. However, he was alone in the room and his friend was working up a ladder in the corridor at the other side of the building.

Holyhead Hotel

There has been an inn on this site since 1520, serving some of the townsfolk who lived in the caves carved into the red sandstone cliffs behind.

When a past landlord first took over the Holyhead Hotel he had already heard rumours that it was haunted. He and his family felt uncomfortable whenever they had to go upstairs, and over a period of eighteen months they would hear a hollow clicking noise, like a light switch being turned on and off. The noise was inexplicable. One bedroom in particular felt chilly. A gentleman who stayed at the hotel for a few months was certain that it was a ghost of a woman, because whenever he felt a presence it was accompanied by the scent of sweet perfume.

When the ground floor was renovated things started to happen as soon as a wall was knocked out in the passageway. Whenever the pub was locked up at night, the last door to be locked was the one next to the passageway. The landlord always felt a cold chill on the back of his neck when locking up for the night.

The most dramatic occurrence happened when the landlord and a friend were in the bar talking one evening after hours. Suddenly they were aware of someone standing behind the bar. The landlord turned round and saw a vague figure. At the same time, his friend cried out that he was on fire and so certain was he that he was enveloped in flames, he frantically tried to put the fire out, beating his clothes wildly. Within a few seconds everything returned to normal. There was no sign of any fire and no history of a fire at the existing building.

The Old Railway Tunnel

The disused railway tunnel which runs under the town is believed to be haunted. During the last war, when the tunnel was still in use, the entrance was guarded by members of the Home Guard. While on guard duty one night a young soldier, Morris Kitchen, saw a ghostly figure coming towards him out of the tunnel. He experienced a feeling of extreme terror, prompting him to aim his rifle at the figure. He remained rooted to the spot for what seemed to be hours as the figure moved closer until vanishing.

Since the closure of the tunnel it has been used as a playground by local children. One bonfire night while playing in the tunnel, a ghostly, brightly coloured figure came towards a group of children. They ran away in terror, vowing never to enter the tunnel again.

During the tunnel's construction a workman was run over by a cart and suffered fatal injuries. Perhaps it is he who walks the tunnel carrying a large oil lamp that glows around the damp tunnel walls?

The Hand

A young lady from Shropshire had a troubled relationship with her aunt who said many unkind and slanderous things about her. The aunt moved to Paris and for sometime they had no contact with one another. Her niece moved to Bridgnorth to stay with some friends.

One day they were out driving in their horse-drawn carriage towards Cleobury North. They were just outside Bridgnorth when suddenly the horse stopped dead and refused to move. The coachman whipped it but still it refused. The young lady then tried to lead the horse. As she did she was flung aside by some unseen force. A gigantic hand and arm materialised holding the horse by the neck. At that moment, a church clock in Bridgnorth began to strike twelve noon. The hand faded and they were able to move on, but were so upset that they had to return home; the horse was never fit for work again. It was a few days later that the young lady learnt that her aunt had died in Paris at noon on the day the ghostly hand stopped her carriage.

The Crown & Raven Hotel (now the Crown)

The Crown & Raven, as it was known, has a ghost of a young woman called Evie who worked at the inn 200 years ago. A woman who claimed to be a medium came to the pub and was unwilling to go into the kitchen. She complained of feeling sick and feeling someone pushing poison down her throat.

A retired landlord of the Crown & Raven never saw Evie, but complained that there was always a lot of noise at night which could not be accounted for, including footsteps on the first and ground floors. The compressed air for the beer would also switch itself off occasionally.

A previous landlady had a few strange experiences, and her two Alsatian dogs would not go into the upstairs flat. They would sit outside the door with their hackles up. The bathroom light in the flat kept switching itself on. One morning, at about 7.30 a.m., she went downstairs. She had employed a man to come in early to do the bottling up. He commented, when she said good morning, that she was more sociable than the young woman he had seen earlier. He said the woman had come in and gone behind the bar and when he spoke to her, she had ignored him. When he was told that there was no one else in the building he went white, realising he had seen the ghost.

A séance was held one evening and they received a message from a young girl. She said she was nineteen years old, named Evie, and was a chambermaid. She was engaged to a man but found out that he was having an affair with someone else, who she killed. Evie was executed for murder but had enjoyed her time at the Crown & Raven and wanted to stay.

Falcon Hotel

The Falcon Hotel is a seventeenth-century coaching inn situated close to the River Severn in Bridgnorth. Some years ago an old man named Willie would often come in at lunchtime with his secretary for lunch. As he left the hotel he would wink and tip the staff and say, 'Don't tell my wife I was here at lunchtime'. This went on for many years, and then he went on a cruise from which he never returned alive. One day one of the ex-members of staff who had known Willie was sitting in the dining room having lunch. She suddenly felt someone standing behind her. Just then the champagne glasses on the Welsh dresser shattered for no reason. She sensed it was Willie because she suddenly found herself saying, 'Of course I won't tell your wife you were here'. When staff came on duty that evening, having replaced all the champagne glasses, the table at which Willie always sat was found with everything disarranged and the glasses broken. What is interesting is that at the top of the list of diners that night were Willie's widow and son!

The Black Boy

The Black Boy is a traditional pub whose pub sign depicts a chimney sweep. It was formerly known as the Prince Charles.

A few years ago the landlord and his wife were watching a late-night film on television when suddenly their five-year-old daughter began screaming from her bedroom upstairs. They rushed upstairs to find their terrified child unable to speak. The next morning, their daughter told them that she awoke to see a woman, dressed in a beautiful blue dress, entering her room. The woman stood by her bed, staring at her. It was not her mother, and the girl hid beneath her bedclothes. Peeking out again, the woman continued to stand and stare. The daughter, by now terrified, screamed until her parents arrived in the room. Ever since then, the landlords have had to keep the lights on to reassure their daughter.

Mrs Brown, a former landlady, remembers entering the far cellar and as she approached the final archway there was a sudden purple flash before her. Startled, she stood and looked at the purple column of light for a moment before it disappeared into the ceiling. Her immediate thought was an electrical surge and she rushed upstairs, fully expecting to find the pub in total darkness. To her surprise everything was normal, though her husband did say that there had been the smell of burning just before he returned.

St James Priory

A leper hospital stood on the site of the house known as St James Priory, outside the town on the east of the road from Bridgnorth to Quatt and south of its junction with the road to Stourbridge; a typical site for such a hospital.

During the Civil War a gypsy was arrested for spying and taken to St James Priory. During her painful interrogation she announced that whoever killed her would be cursed, and so would their family. To overcome this, her interrogators decided to entomb her in one of the small rooms in the cellar and brick her in. A few months later the room was re-opened and they expected to find her body. Nothing was found and no explanation could be found as to how she had got out – the brick wall had still been intact. It was not until the late 1800s that a roughly bricked-up alcove was found containing the skeleton of a young woman and a newborn baby. They were re-buried following a christening service in the grounds.

When the Priory closed in 1957 the owner continued to live in a nearby cottage. One Saturday the doorbell rang and the housekeeper went to the door. There was no one there. As she went to close the door, she felt a horrible gust of wind rush past her. The owner's dog began to bark and his hair stood on end and appeared to follow the gusting wind through the house. The gardener, who was at the back door, was almost blown off his feet by the force of the gust as it exited the cottage. Many visitors to the priory before its demolition sensed they

The gypsy lady.

were being watched, and often would only visit the once, never to return. One local man recalled the experience of his late uncle who worked at the priory and every evening would set off and collect the newspaper for the owner. As he entered the cottage through the back door he suddenly became very cold, shivered and dropped the paper. He bent down to recover it and when standing back up, was amazed by a figure of white floating through the trees. It was a young girl with long dark hair who smiled as she passed before floating away into the trees.

He sat down in the kitchen for a few moments to recover, then went to tell the mistress of the house of his experience. He entered the library with her newspaper under his arm and walked over to her sitting by the fire. As he rounded the chair he realised she was dead. It wasn't until later that he found a book in the library about the family where he found the following passage, 'When the head of the family dies in the Priory the ghost of a young girl, dressed in white, will be seen floating through the trees in the Priory grounds'.

Gallows Field

Last used for executions in 1767 when John Scott Haines was tied up in chains to starve to death for the attempted murder of Joseph Boat, a tailor of West Castle street. The chained body of a man hanging from a long-gone tree has been seen followed by a deep-seated sick feeling as the image fades.

Bridgnorth Station

Bridgnorth Station is a grand stone edifice in the Jacobean style. The line opened in 1862 and operated for 101 years until 1963. After years of neglect following the cuts to many branch lines, the station at Bridgnorth saw new life in the form of the Severn Valley Railway Company and re-opened in 1970. It was only when the line reopened that ghostly figures were seen of a man wearing Edwardian clothing, holding the hand of his daughter dressed in the same period style with a large straw hat with long ribbons trailing from it. They have been seen in the day waving at approaching trains, with visitors believing them to be part of living history projects – that is until told the truth that they have seen the ghosts of the station. Were they waiting for a mother and wife to return to the station? Had they died on the way to the station? All we do know is the man and the girl like to appear on busy days to wave at the trains arriving.

Innage, Bridgnorth

In 1929, whilst walking his dog before he went to bed, Mr Cyril Lloyd became aware that his dog was watching and growling at something ahead of them. There were no street lights and his torch was weak, but he pointed it towards the area at which the dog was barking. Mr Lloyd then saw a man dressed in a cape and a trilby-type hat on. The figure drifted across the path before disappearing through a garden wall. That night his dog had a very short walk!

The Acton Burnell Ghost

During a ghost hunt of the ruins by a group of students, a ghostly apparition made an appearance to one of the group, Stuart, who was so taken with the apparition that he nearly

Acton Burnell Castle.

forgot to take pictures. The few he took show a grey figure of a woman near a doorway and orbs. He also felt someone, with a gentle touch, standing next to him. His photographs were later shown on BBC Shropshire website and Stuart insists that they are genuine.

The ghost is believed to be Sara, a young daughter of Mr Smythe who owned the castle in the seventeenth century. Sara was out on a ride with her companion when a fox shot out of the hedge and caused her horse to bolt, throwing her to the ground where she broke her neck. She was dressed in her favourite outfit of white lace for her burial. Soon after, the castle was abandoned and fell into ruin.

Wilderhope Manor

The most famous of the resident ghosts is Major Smallman himself, who has been seen by many people, staff and visitors alike. One sighting was recorded in the *Shropshire Magazine* by a Mr Crane who was painting the ceiling in one of the ground floor rooms as part of his payment to stay at the hostel. As he painted the left of the plaster ceiling, he became aware of someone watching him. From the corner of his eye, he saw a figure that had been watching him for a while but thought it was the warden overseeing his work to ensure its quality. He looked down at the doorway and saw a tall man:

> wearing a green cloak, a brown hat with a long white plume and leather boots that reached to his thighs. His shirt had ruffles at the throat and he wore a sword. He was looking directly at me. I was too awed to feel fear or any emotion apart from curiosity about this splendid character. I tried desperately to think of an apt remark but only uttered "Good day". As I spoke, he raised his left hand and smiled. He then proceeded to walk towards the further wall, then with another smile, he walked straight through the solid wall.

Mr Crane left the hostel the following day, excited that he had met the Wilderhope ghost.

Wilderhope Manor.

St Peters Church, Stanton Lacy

The original church of St Peter's was built on the orders of the King of Mercia, Penda, after his daughter, Milburga, was saved from a Welsh prince who was trying to capture and murder her. Chased to a small wood at Stanton Lacy, she hid and prayed that the River Cove would swell and become impassable. Her prayers were answered and the Prince, unable to reach her, gave up his chase. A church was founded on the site in AD 680 to honour God's answer to Milburga's prayers.

The ghost of a churchwarden frequents the church. He was murdered for refusing to let Cromwell's marauding troops enter. He knew that, as with other churches in the area, they would desecrate the church and steal anything of value. He ended his days on the end of a pike in front of the church as a deterrent to any would-be defenders. Cromwell's troops ransacked the church but failed to find the few treasures it possessed and soon moved on. During burials in the churchyard, he watches over the proceedings, as he would have done when he was alive. If you should approach and in any way resemble his bloody assassins, he will force you from the church. Some people have felt giddy and nauseous and experienced the terrifying feeling of a hand pushed flat on their chest to push them away from the church.

Hopton Castle

The castle is of great historical interest as it was given to Walter de Opton (later Hopton) of Clifford Castle, Herefordshire, by Henry II. By 1286, it was in the possession of Roger, Lord Mortimer of Chirk.

For many years the castle, built as a border station against the Welsh, saw little action. The focus of uprising tended to be at nearby Clun. It was not until the Civil War that this once fine castle saw real fighting, and was blown apart by Cromwell's men who were on the rampage in the area. The garrison of thirty-three men and their commander, Colonel Samuel More, held the Royalists off for weeks. When all their food was finished and the gunpowder supply had run out, only then did the colonel strike a deal with the commanding officer of the Roundheads. They would surrender the castle and instead of facing death, they agreed to being imprisoned.

The commanding officer of the Roundheads agreed to the deal saying that the colonel should come out first so that he could oversee his men being fed and watered. Colonel Samuel More was reluctant to do this but eventually walked across the drawbridge and into the hands of the Roundheads. With his captors holding a knife across his throat he was told to call his men out one by one. As his men came out of the castle they were beheaded, one by one, in front of him and their bodies unceremoniously kicked into the moat. Their heads were mounted on stakes atop of the castle to stare lifelessly at the now-distraught Colonel More. More was taken to Ludlow Castle, dragged behind the commander's horse, after he was forced to watch as Hopton Castle was blown up.

To this day, the atrocious crime of the Civil War in Shropshire is acted out on moonlit nights. People passing Hopton Castle have seen the men file out, one by one, and their heads disappear before their bodies fall away into the now-dry moat.

Hopton Castle ruins.

Chapel Farm, Clunbury

The old chapel at Clunbury now forms part of the farmhouse. It used to be the only chapel for miles around and served the local community of farmers and their families. For many years, the chapel held Sunday evening services run by passing clerics. That was until strange noises started to be heard from inside and outside the chapel during the service. To begin with, people put it down to the wind, rain or just the movement of animals in the fields surrounding the chapel. After a few months the noise was so great that the passing clerics complained of not being heard. The congregation stopped turning up for the evening services, preferring to go to other chapels or churches. Eventually the chapel was closed. Despite this, some of the hill farmers noticed strange lights and noises coming from inside the chapel. As soon as they got close enough to investigate, everything went dark and quiet. If they were brave enough to enter, nothing would be found. Local rumour said it was the Devil who was holding meetings.

The chapel finally fell into disrepair and it was incorporated in 1853 into the farmhouse. There have been no noises heard, although a tall grey figure has been seen in the area inside the house that would have once been the chapel.

Plaish Hall, Cardington

Plaish Hall is Elizabethan, with outstanding examples of Tudor chimneys. It was built on the site of a much smaller, and earlier, manor house. The original house was built of stone, but the owner, Judge Leighton, Chief Justice of the Principality of Wales, remodelled Plaish Hall in brick.

With the work almost complete, he searched for a chimney builder to add the last grand ornamental touches. The only person capable of building the ornate brick chimneys had been sentenced to be hanged by the judge himself the day before.

Judge Leighton (known as the Hanging Judge) spent some time with the man in his cell, convincing him that if he built the chimneys he would let him walk free. His wife and children begged their father to accept the offer, fearing his execution planned for the next morning. The man agreed to do the work and moved to the hall with his family to start on the chimneys. Halfway through the building works, the judge also found a job for his wife in a nearby village and work for the children on farms nearby. Little did they know of the wicked Judges Leighton's plans.

When the chimneys were finished, the judge thanked the builder and said he was free to go… to the gallows. The evil judge had never intended to keep his promise and had the convict – as he saw him – hung from the chimneys he had worked so painstakingly to build. To cover his actions, Judge Leighton bricked the body up in one of the chimney cavities.

Before he died, the man cursed the judge and the house saying that no good would ever come to those who reside at Plaish Hall. The man's wife visited the hall to find out the whereabouts of her husband only to be told, by servants, that he had gone off two days before saying he wanted to be with his wife and family.

Since his death, the man has been seen hanging from the chimneys, walking the gardens with his hangman's noose in hand, and on the driveway where he has been blamed for the death of a father who returned home to the hall one night ahead of his wife and children. This father was a good driver and had not been drinking and no one can explain why he drove down the drive at such speed before crashing in to a large tree. His wife and children witnessed the accident and saw a figure standing beside the burning car.

One of the most frightening signs of his presence is that of blood oozing out of the chimney breasts, appearing as handprints on the furniture and on the floors. The figure of a man and woman haunt the Great Hall. High up in the attic, on the floor, is said to be a burn left by the hooves of the Devil where he tricked some greedy men to play cards one Sunday. The Devil took their souls by whisking them up in a whirlwind scattering tables, chairs and bodies.

During some alterations on the second floor in 1916, the skeletal remains of a male with a noose was discovered bricked up in a chimneybreast where much of the apparent 'blood' was coming from.

Squire Blount of Kinlet

Sir George Blount, Squire Blount as he preferred, was a great soldier and during the Scottish Wars became known as the 'Terror of Scotland'. He did not suffer fools gladly. When his daughter announced that she was to marry a man he did not approve of, he disinherited her and gave all his worldly goods to his wife. He died in 1581, having lost his young son who choked on an apple, aged just five. As he lay dying his wife told him she was going to give the inheritance back to his daughter. He was so angry he vowed that if she did, he would haunt them both forever. His coffin was placed alongside the silver coffin of his son inside a fine example of an Elizabethan stone carved tomb. The tomb can be seen in the church.

Squire Blunt haunted the district within a week of the funeral. He was seen to rise up from the pool in the formal grounds of Kinlet Hall, ride a horse back through the walls and terrorise guests sitting down for lunch.

Heath House

Over twenty years ago, there was a notorious murder in Shropshire that caused ripples through the whole county and beyond. Heath House at Hopton Heath was the home of Simon Dale, a reclusive architect who was convinced that the area around the house had links to King Arthur and the Holy Grail. He believed both were buried in the grounds of Heath House. Giselle Wall, Simon's research assistant, discovered the body of Simon Dale by the back door in the kitchen with his head smashed in by a blunt instrument. Toad-in-the-hole was still cooking in the oven and there were signs that there had been a struggle in the kitchen.

Simon Dale's estranged wife, Susan, was a regular visitor to Heath House and believed that much of the furniture, and indeed the property, was hers by right.

Police immediately followed up reports that Susan had been seen with two of her children, Marcus and Sophie, outside Heath House, and had broken in to the property to take furniture she claimed was hers. This caused arguments with Simon who, being partly sighted, was not always aware she was in the building. Did she murder him because she demanded the house be put up for sale following their divorce in 1972? After all, she had waited fifteen years and possibly had had enough of his obsession with Camelot, King Arthur and the Holy Grail which Simon had claimed was under the house due to his discovery of thick stone walls and a wide street under the lawns. After a trial, Susan was acquitted of any offence to do with the murder of Simon Dale.

A number of sightings have since been made of Simon Dale walking across the lawn of the house, looking at the ground. There was a sighting of someone of good build, and balding, in the kitchen when work was being done to upgrade the house.

Before the Dales moved in, a very angry husband, whose wife was dying of cancer after being wrongly diagnosed by Dr Beach, the local GP, lured the doctor to the house. As he reached the top of the long drive, Dr Beach leant over to secure his bag and turned back to face the house when he was shot dead.

Roberry Ring

Dilys Knight had a strange experience when she was visiting her parents near Roberry Ring. In a letter to the author, she wrote:

> From 1945 to 1962 my parents lived at Pear Tree Cottage, Prolley Moor, near Wenton. My husband and I having taken over the family business on their retirement we visited them every Easter, Whitsun and August Bank holiday together with our son and dog Caen. I did not 'believe' in ghosts at that time, being quite convinced they were imagined or had a rational explanation. It was one Easter time, there were no leaves on the trees, one evening my son

was in bed, my husband declined to accompany me, and I took the dog for a walk. I walked as per the map below up the road on a level with Roberry Ring then retraced my steps as it was approaching dusk. As I approached the cross roads I heard what sounded like a horse galloping along the road to my right going in the direction of Asterton, as the dog was running free I called him to me and held his collar; the sound became louder and to my surprise it looked like a man in a cloak riding furiously, his cloak and the horses tail flowing out behind them. With shock I noticed that I could see the bare hedge through them! The sound of the hooves died away in the distance towards Asterton. Had not been reading or thinking about ghosts and could not believe what I had experienced, but it left me with a feeling of concern, which persisted.

I have since made many enquiries but no one local had seen this rider or could throw any light on why I had seen him.

Astley Abbots

Leaving Bridgnorth on the road to Broseley is the village of Astley Abbots, where two ghosts appear in the same area.

The first is that of Hannah Phillips, who was due to get married in the church but never made it. She had gone to the church with her family to get it ready for her wedding the next day. Her mother, father and sisters had gone ahead as Hannah waited for her elderly aunt to arrive. Her aunt arrived and settled, Hannah went off to the church. She was never seen alive again. Some believe she slipped at the ford and was drowned in the sunken cave just down the river where her small clutch bag was found in a shallow pool. Locals report having seen Hannah's ghost walking from her former home to the river – but never beyond. One driver saw her walking along the road before she turned and glided in front of his car towards the river.

Twenty years earlier, Mr Tipton of Astley Abbots reported seeing a man walking towards him as he cycled to Colemore Green. He was intrigued by the man as he wore a Sunday best suit and had a white flower in the button hole of his jacket. As Mr Tipton came closer, the man faded into the surrounding hedge.

Nearby, at Boldings Farm, there is a ghost building that appears on hot summer days for a minute or two before vanishing from view.

The Ghost of Mary Way

Between Bridgnorth and Much Wenlock is the small hamlet of Muckley Cross, with many timber-framed cottages bearing a cross in low relief dated 1708. The monks of the abbey at Much Wenlock had a field, or lay (meadow), hence its earlier name of Monk-ley Cross.

The ghost that haunts Muckley Cross is that of a young local woman, Mary Way, who was assaulted by two travellers as she walked home from work. Mary Way was subjected to a violent rape before having her head cut off and thrown into a nearby hedge. When Mary failed to return home that night, a search party gathered and the two men were found nearby with

Hannah Phillips, near
the river.

blood splattered over their coats and trousers. It took a few days for the men to finally confess
to the bloody murder, for which they were hanged in the gaol at Shrewsbury.

For many years after the murder, the figure of a tall headless woman, Mary Way, has been
reported. Since the arrival of the motor car the sightings have become less frequent – perhaps
due to the speed passing the site of the haunting compared with that from a horse drawn
coach.

Major's Leap

Thomas Smallman was a major in the Royalist Army during the Civil War who lived at
Wilderhope, on Wenlock Edge. It was whilst he was away from his home that a group of
Cromwell's troopers came upon the hall having escaped from the battle of Worcester. They
overpowered and bound the two remaining servants to chairs in the dining room and made off
with silver and gold objects as booty. The major arrived soon after and went in pursuit along
the road to Ludlow. Such was the swiftness of his attack that he managed to kill several of the
troopers before regaining his belongings.

On a later occasion, Major Smallman was carrying dispatches for his Royal Master from
Bridgnorth to Shrewsbury when he was ambushed as he rode into his stable yard at Wilderhope.
The Roundheads secured him in an attic space with a guard posted outside, while the rest
talked in the parlour, drinking ale and eating to excess. What they did not know was that the
room in which they had imprisoned the major had a secret trapdoor through which he could
escape to the ground floor. When all was quiet, Major Smallman made his escape down the
ladder, through the secret door and out to the stable where he saddled his horse. The Royal
dispatches had remained safe in a secret saddle pocket. The major tried to ride off quietly but
was quickly spotted by the Roundheads. They raced behind him and were about to catch him

when he made a drastic decision – to ride over the Wenlock Edge. He pulled off the road to Much Wenlock and rode to the large, flat stone now known as Major's Leap and raced full pelt over the edge, some 200ft high. Into the abyss he and his horse fell and it was only a crab apple tree leaning out from the base of the cliff that saved him. His horse perished but Major Smallman survived and made it to Shrewsbury on foot to deliver the dispatches.

To this day, the whole scene is recreated when the hooves of a horse are heard clattering along the road, then the thundering as the horse and rider go off road before the loud shout and the noise of a heavy object falling through the trees below the Major's Leap. Some claim to have seen just the horse leaping from the rock, whilst others have seen both horse and rider.

Old Ippikin

Between Presthope and Lutwyche Hall on Wenlock Edge is a great rock known as Ippikin's Rock. It is named after a highwayman, or robber knight, named Ippikin who roamed the roads leading to Much Wenlock in order to rob the riches of travellers. Records suggest that Ippikin was a monk from the Abbey in Much Wenlock with fiery red hair and a long chin who turned to crime when he found that he could not cope with the reclusive life of a monk. Others believed he and his men were wizards, able to renew life every seventy years. Ippikin was a rogue with a fierce temper that would erupt without warning. He had a sense of justice, for he would steal from the rich only, letting the poor travel in peace. His riches and treasures were stored in his cave at Ippikin's Rock. One day, returning from a robbery, he was struck by lightning as he entered his cave below the top of the rock, fatally trapping him inside. Today screams can be heard as Ippikin tried in vain to escape his tomb.

Local legend has it that if you try to find the treasures stored by Ippikin, his spirit is sure to push you off the rock as he jealously guards his store.

Recite the following rhyme and you are sure to meet Ippikin:

Ippikin, Ippikin, Keep away with your long chin…Ippikin.

Old Ippikin.

His enraged spirit will be summoned, and his men will rush from their graves, to push those foolish enough to tempt him forth to their sure death over the cliff.

Wenlock Edge

Wenlock Edge was part of a large hunting estate. There was a gamekeeper and many under keepers to patrol the hunting grounds for poachers. One under keeper was plagued by a family well-known for poaching, and whilst he never caught them, he instinctively knew they were on his patch. One night when there was a half moon he sat waiting for the poachers to visit his pheasant pens as they had done the night before, making off with 100 of his birds. On hearing a muffled shot nearby, the under keeper went off to catch the poachers. He caught up with two men and a struggle took place at Cross Banks, Wenlock Edge. A shotgun was discharged into the under keeper's chest. He was still alive, and the poachers hatched a plan to take him close to a road to be found and hopefully saved. They dragged his body for a while before they realised he had died, so left him under a hedge alongside the Much Wenlock to Church Stretton road. They each made their way home as it began to snow. This was their downfall, or at least for one of them, as the trail led police to the home of the elder poacher who would not tell police who the other poacher was. He claimed he had just met him as he walked through the woods.

He confessed to accidentally shooting the under keeper when he made a grab for the poacher's sawn-off shotgun. The police pushed for the name of the other person but in the end gave up and the former poacher was executed for his part in the death of the under keeper.

Ever since the body was found that area of hedge has lain barren, with no plants or trees growing and any fence erected has been smashed down that same night. The only thing that has stayed in place is a gate – known as the clattering glat – because at night it is heard to clatter furiously as if to summon help.

Be careful when driving along Wenlock Edge at Cross Banks where there is the ghost of a man who is seen to walk along the road on summer evenings. As you approach him he may suddenly step out right in front of you, causing you to crash or drive straight through him. He is seen at the Plough Inn near the car park for Ippikin's rock. A little further down the road, towards Much Wenlock, is part of a ghost road that follows the original route of the road before it was diverted to allow part of the edge to be quarried. At night, often with fog around, the ghost road appears, luring drivers up a bank on what was the original line of the old road that leads to a high plunge into the quarry below. To prevent death and injury, the council have erected concrete barriers to stop such accidents so thankfully only pride and a few cars have been harmed.

Easthope Manor

Easthope Manor was once a farm, part of the Wenlock Abbey estate, and the scene of a double killing when two monks from the abbey fought over gold they had amassed from local traders. Whilst they were counting their gold coins a dispute started and ended with the pair rolling about the ground floor before plunging down the stairs to the cellar. The two monks were found with their necks broken, surrounded by some of their gold.

Easthope Manor.

They were buried with half of the gold. The rest, if the story is true, went to the abbot. A few months after the monks were buried, a local man thought the gold would be better in his pocket and went to the grave one night, prised the large stone cover off the grave, before suddenly dropping dead. The stone fell to the ground and split in two. It can still be seen with the great crack in it. The ghosts of the two monks are seen fighting around the grave with savage force, sufficient to put off would-be thieves trying to steal the gold that remains buried beneath the stone slab.

The monks are also seen and heard in the half timber-framed manor house of Easthope where a plaster ceiling bears the motto '*Droit Est Mal Mer*' translated from old French meaning 'Lawful right is ill moved'. The same can be found at Wilderhope Manor in the large hall.

St Peter's Church, Easthope

The ghost of William Garmston haunts St Peter's Church at Easthope after he was murdered there by John de Easthope, the patron, for reading very long sermons. In 1333, Garmston's skull was broken. Soon after, John de Easthope committed suicide.

Garmston is known to appear as a short grey figure by the side of newcomers to the village. His spirit is familiar rather than threatening.

Lutwyche Hall, near Easthope

The name of the first building recorded on the site, now known as Lutwyche Hall, was recorded in *The Domesday Book* as 'The Lotesis'. The present hall, built for J.E. Lutwytch in 1587. The hall features fine plaster decoration, and Victorian Jacobean-style trim with later additions to include grand Italian designs to the walls and ceilings.

The hall is believed to be the oldest brick building in Shropshire, constructed months before Plaish Hall which was built for Judge Leighton.

Lutwyche Hall.

The ghost that haunts Lutwyche Hall is said to be that of the late Judge Edward Lutwyche accompanied by either his old housekeeper or mother – no one can be sure. Their favourite trick is to move furniture around the main rooms when the owners are asleep upstairs. One incident was recorded when a family moved in and for three days in succession, all the furniture in the sitting and drawing rooms were rearranged in a traditional seventeenth-century way. The family were not unsurprisingly worried; was one of them sleep-walking and moving furniture in their sleep? It was not until the neighbour popped in to see how the family were getting on and asked if the furniture was staying put that the family felt they could express their concerns.

The neighbour explained that following the death of Judge Lutwyche when new people moved in to the hall (even the heir), it was commonplace for furniture to move. This would happen for three to four days. They all laughed with relief and sure enough, as the neighbour said, on the fourth day the furniture was never moved again by any ghostly hand.

The judge and his older companion are seen walking the corridors of the hall checking off a list, and in the grounds, looking back at the hall. All who have seen them feel that the ghosts were making sure that the hall remains cherished and cared for.

Morville

Throughout the country are a number of ghost houses. At Morville there is a large country house that appears high up on the hill overlooking Morville. A garden party is in full swing. The guests are dressed in Victorian or Edwardian costume taking high tea, with great aunts watching the children play and servants coming and going. Yet, within minutes of the house being visible, it bursts into flames before the vision disappears. There are no records of a building being on the site and no explanation as to why it should appear.

The Devil's Talon

Outside the village of Minsterley is a fine timber-framed building that once saw one of the strangest events in Shropshire. In the Georgian period it was owned by a gentleman who had arrived, he claimed, after making his fortune abroad, returning to Shropshire to enjoy the company of friends. He found the house had just been put up for sale after the previous owner had passed away. The new owner had his belongings shipped in from Italy and London and soon his residence was the talk of the area. His wealth continued to amass and he was the envy of many. Rumours soon started that he must have sold his soul to the Devil for such wealth.

One Christmas Eve he staged the largest, most extravagant party ever seen in Shropshire and invited all of his friends, including many of the county's aristocracy. They had all eaten well and as was tradition at the end of a meal the women retired to the music room, leaving the men to their drinking, smoking and cards. Suddenly there was an unearthly noise coming from the long avenue of trees to the house. It sounded like a disembodied scream of, 'You are mine!' as the noise came closer. There was panic in the room and the men, looking out of the windows, saw a fiery, tall red figure rushing towards the house. There was more panic and commotion as the men fled through any door they could find, followed in quick pursuit by the women. The party huddled as the house was engulfed with a bright red and yellow glow that shot through all the windows and out through the chimneys. As suddenly as it started the commotion came to an end.

They returned to the house and could not believe the utter destruction. To their consternation they found the owner had gone missing. The butler went instinctively to the dining room where he found him dead beneath an upturned table with great gashes to his clothes and body. When the body was checked for signs of life by a doctor he found a large talon embedded in the eye of the victim. Was it from the Devil or some demon calling in a loan?

The Devil's Talon.

Stiperstones and the
Devil's Chair.

The Devil's Chair

'A thunderstorm instantly arises and on the longest night of the year all the ghosts in Shropshire meet on Stiperstones highest point to choose their king.' It is said that on the shortest day all the ghosts of England appear on the Stiperstones around the Devil's Chair for a party and to see who the new souls the Devil has caught are, with the Devil watching from his worldly throne.

Wild Edric

Wild Edric, or Edric the Wild, was a Saxon leader who led the revolt against the Norman invaders during the eleventh century. His real name was Edric Sylvatius and he lived for many years as lord of much of the Shropshire hills around the Stiperstones.

Edric had great power and was known to be a brave man who lived up to his reputation for being wild. But he was also a fair and just man. He loved to hunt around the Long Mynd, the Stiperstones and especially through the great Forest of Cund.

It was at the end of a day of hunting that Edric found himself alone with his horse, making his way through the forest. He rode for a while and slowly became aware of the sound of music. Following its source he came to a clearing and a solitary cottage. Looking in the window he saw seven maidens dancing. As his eyes rested upon the maiden in the centre, the most beautiful of them all, he was filled with love and knew she would become his bride. He seized the young beautiful girl and made off to Lydbury.

Back in his manor house the girl remained silent. On the third day she finally spoke:

I know who you are, you are Edric, the one they call the Wild, but I have watched you these days and I have not seen a wild man but rather one straight and true, and I know you would marry me. Well, I will marry you but first you must know who I am. My name is Godda and I am the Queen of the fairy folk and it is from my six sister fairies that you have stolen me, but

I will marry you and live with you the life of a human, provided you never reproach me. You must never reproach me with who I am, where you found me or with my sisters from whom you stole me. Should you do so I'll return to fairy land and you'll never see me again. Now, do you swear?'

Edric swore the oath as Godda wished and the two of them married and lived as man and wife. The whole of Shropshire knew of Wild Edric and of his fairy wife Godda.

Wild Edric and his men captured Richard's castle from the Norman invaders in 1069 and moved on to capture Shrewsbury Castle and Shrewsbury town. The castle eventually fell to the invaders and the townspeople surrendered. Edric and a few of his men fled to the nearby woods.

After his capture in 1070 by William the Conqueror, Edric and his fellow men were made an offer of land and income. Whilst the report of Edric's death was circulated around the Shropshire hills in order to bring the rebellion under control, Edric's men knew he was alive, living in one of the many, deep Roman silver mines in the area. This was corroborated by the stories of miners who claimed the best silver seam was to be found where they could hear knocking. They believed it was Edric showing them the way to the silver in order to create enough goodwill to escape his self-imposed imprisonment with his fairy wife Godda. There they lived happily and had a son, Alned, son of the fairy wife. All should have been well, but one day Edric made his mistake. It had become accepted between them that Godda would serve his breakfast and on that day she was just a minute or two late. When she came into the room Edric, in a fit of temper, shouted, 'Where have you been wife? Was it your sisters kept you from me?' The moment he said the words of reproach he remembered his vow, but it was too late. Godda vanished from his sight and he never saw her again when alive.

From that day he was a wild man and rode with his hounds, hunting for his beloved Godda, but he never found her and he died, not long after, a sad and broken man. Although he died, the hunt continued and to this day, his ghost still rides the wild hunt through those Shropshire hill – still hunting for his beloved fairy wife.

Ratlinghope.

Stokesay Castle.

Edric and his fairy wife Godda are said to ride out when there is war coming to our shores and they were last seen riding out to the south, in the direction of the Falklands. In the past they were seen before the outbreak of the Napoleonic War, again in 1854 at the outbreak of the Crimean War, and in 1914 before the outbreak of the First World War. Godda can be seen dressed in a green habit belted with gold and her hair of flowing gold. Edric carries a huge sword and rides a fine warhorse, followed by his many Saxon warriors. Wild Edric and Godda have not been seen of late so perhaps he has served his time and he and Godda have entered their chosen kingdom.

Ratlinghope

In Ratlinghope a ghostly funeral procession can be seen, led by a man in a tall hat with a walking stick followed by the horse-drawn hearse. The long line of mourners follows. Many who have seen the procession have been said to have been drinking in the Horseshoe Inn, with sceptics quick to put the whole sighting down to a drop too much to drink.

However, during a visit to Shropshire a vicar from Brighton was enjoying a walk around the churchyard when he witnessed the procession. The day was bright but as the funeral passed, he noticed a strange mist that appeared to engulf them. When he returned to his friend's house for supper he recounted the spectacle and asked whom the person was who had such a following. His friend went pale before recounting the story of the Devil who regularly brings the souls of the dammed through the hamlet, and how lucky he was to have not been taken too with the lost souls that follow the procession. Unsurprisingly, the vicar never returned to Shropshire.

Stokesay Castle

Legend has it that there were giant twins who lived either side of the valley, one on View Edge and the other at Norton Camp. They shared their riches equally and used the same safe to keep their money in. They sold livestock, timber and made a fortune from charging passing travellers a toll to pass through their valley. One day the Norton giant needed the key and so bellowed across to his twin for it. It was thrown, yet fell short of the mark, falling into the moat of Stokesay Castle where it was lost forever. The twins searched to no avail for the key and trained a large raven to watch over their money whilst they went off to find the locksmith who made them the lock. They were never to return and the raven is still guarding their money until the end of time. So next time you are at the castle, watch out for the raven who may decide you are too close to the twin's treasure.

Michell's Fold Stone Circle, Lydham

During times of drought or hardship, a white cow would appear in the middle of the circle and allow everyone in the neighbourhood to fill one bucket with milk. Michell, a local witch after whom the circle named, milked the cow into a sieve until the creature vanished. She kept the cow for herself and it was only released after her death. The magic cow was so worn out it died shortly after the witch. To this day the white cow has been seen around the outside of the circle, but never again has it been seen inside the circle.

Presthope

A headless horseman is seen in the area riding towards the Longmynd, and on one occasion he made such an impact on a young farmer who saw him that his hair went straight!

In 1979 it was fashionable to have a crinkle hair perm and the young farmer was going to show off his new perm to friends. As he walked across a field towards Presthope he heard the noise of a horse galloping from behind. Looking back he could not see anything, but the sound of thundering hooves continued. Without warning an image of a headless horseman bounded out of the darkness. He fell to the ground thinking he was going to be hit by the horse. There was no impact. Thinking himself lucky to have escaped and still in shock, he rushed on to meet his friends who were eagerly waiting to see his new hair do. To his astonishment, his hair was straighter than ever when he reached the pub and stayed that way for weeks to come.

The Seven Whistlers

As with many legends around the country there are many that predict the end of the world, and Shropshire is no exception. There are six birds seen on the Stiperstones who whistle a tune together. When there are seven birds and they sing together it is a sign that the end of the world is coming.

The Willows, Bucknell, Craven Arms

The Willows is a delightful fifteenth-century cruck-framed house that has a tea room and guest house. On a summer day it seems idyllic, yet go inside and you may change your mind. The ghost is not an unhappy one, but is a little mischievous. He appears as solid as a real guest before vanishing. He is often seen on the landing and is so convincing that guests have moved to one side in order to let him pass. He is a tall man with a large Victorian moustache, in a smoking jacket and carrying a pipe from which the smell of sandalwood emanates.

Witch of Westwood Common

On 12 September 1857, Thomas Yates, the local barber and constable found sixty-nine-year-old Nan Morgan lying dead in her cottage on Westwood Common, stabbed in the face, neck and wrist. The constable had been called because some children walking across the common heard screams and then saw a man, later identified as Mr William Davies, leaving the cottage with what looked like blood all over his clothing.

Anne (Nan) Morgan was in service at Bourton Hall where she was caught stealing from the family and sent to prison for a year. After prison she had nothing and after a chance meeting with a gypsy woman, she stayed with her and trained in the art of making poison, weaving spells and reading fortunes. On leaving the gypsy, fully trained, she found the near derelict cottage on the common and set about making it her home. She was popular and was visited by many who were looking to know their future. She was often paid in gold or jewellery.

A young farm labourer fell under her charms and lodged with her for payment in kind. He was half her age and wanted to break away but she was a very domineering woman. One day he visited Wenlock for a drink with a woman his own age. When he returned Nan was angry with him as she had found out about his secret tryst. He packed his bag and picked up a watch she had given him. Nan wanted it back. There was a struggle and, fearing for his life as she came at him, he drew his knife and stabbed her to death before fleeing. In the cottage, signs of a frenzied struggle were obvious. The table and chairs were upturned and all manner of items associated with witchcraft were strewn across the floor – cats, toads, potions, wands etc.

Believing her to be a witch, Nan Morgan was buried in the clothes she died in without a service, her cottage burnt to the ground, the jewellery and money seized by the courts for the poor of the parish. Her tools of witchcraft were publicly burnt by order of the Mayor under the watchful eye of the town crier.

William Davies was sentenced to death but this was commuted to transportation to Australia. Many people lived in fear of Nan Morgan, the witch, and were pleased to see her out of the way for good. Or so they thought. The small figure of Nan Morgan is seen on Westwood Common beckoning young men towards her. If you approach it is said that you will love no other for the rest of your life and meet her in eternity.

Longnor Pool

Though the name remains, the pool has long been filled in due to the tragic events that took place one warm summer night in the 1860s. A stream still runs through the village and at the bridge over Longnor brook is where the White Lady is seen. In 1881 she was seen by a local man who was known to be pushy with the local women; married or not, he did not seem to worry. He saw the beautiful young woman standing near the brook looking across the fields and crept up on her and made a grab for her waist. Imagine his horror when his hands passed straight through her. She turned her head, smiled, then vanished. He never made an unwanted pass at a woman after that.

The White Lady has been seen on other occasions along the road to Shrewsbury and is partial to appearing at local dances where she is seen dancing to her heart's content – just don't try to hold her or she vanishes.

The local community are proud of their White Lady and believe she was a village girl who lost her intended husband in battle and committed suicide in Longnor Pool on the eve of what was to have been her wedding day.

The Hurst, Cleobury Mortimer

A young family moved into a semi detached house that had been empty for a while and set about redecorating. Upstairs, as they stripped away layers of wallpaper and paint, they discovered a sealed up door to a room. On the outside of the house there were four windows facing the road, yet inside just three. It did not take long to open the door and for light to flood the room. The children liked it so much that they decided that it would be their bedroom. Two days after opening up the room the father was in the garden and looked up to see a man standing at the window. Rushing into the house he ran upstairs and into the room. No one could be found and the back door remained locked from the inside. Soon after, he heard someone in the attic and grabbing a piece of wood, he went to investigate. As he reached for the door the noise of footsteps and the sound of a trunk being dragged across the floor abruptly stopped. He switched on the light and went in. Again, other than a few of their own boxes there was nothing and no one else up there. He told his wife what had happened and they decided not to tell the children. A week later the mother heard the children giggling and a girl's voice. Since they only had sons, this was a surprise. She went into their bedroom to see her boys in mid-air flying in a circle being held up by an invisible force which, in a split-second, let go causing them to crash to the floor. Her sons described a young girl who had been visiting them from her hiding place in the wall. She made them feel happy and was described as being surrounded by bright lights. The boys pointed to where the girl appears, yet it was just the parting wall with the next door cottage. The girl continued to visit the boys.

As winter set in, the parting wall began to feel damp and wallpaper started to peel off in one area. As it peeled off it pulled plaster off the wall in lumps to reveal another hidden door. The father was starting to suspect there might be the remains of the ghost girl. Indeed, a secret room between the two cottages was revealed. It had no windows inside with an access hatch up to the attic that was later found to be bolted above the hatch. There were scratch marks on the back of the door and signs of a candle or oil lamp being used, a well-thumbed Victorian children's picture book and a small headless doll in tatters. From that point on, the noises in the attic got worse, the banging louder and the little girl appeared all over the house, especially wherever the book and doll were placed.

The family could not put up with the haunting any more and left. A few months later another family rented the cottage but they had moved out within two months claiming the cottage was haunted.

The Bull Inn, Ludlow

The Bull Inn is, at its centre, the oldest timber-framed building in Ludlow and is linked to the church by a tunnel that many thought was just an old wives' tale. Whilst refurbishment was going on at the Bull in the 1980s, a priest hole was discovered in one of the large chimneys breasts. It is a little over 5ft in height and well made. Further work uncovered a set of steps cut into the same chimney leading to a blocked-off door opening. Was this the entrance to the tunnel?

Mr Chris Barrack, a previous landlord, told of his experiences at the Bull. He remembers that two months after they had moved in, on a Sunday at around 7 p.m., he was downstairs opening up on his own. He was standing at the till waiting for his first customer when he felt a hand firmly hold his shoulder and he turned thinking it was his wife. No one was there. He called his wife on the intercom who said she had been upstairs all the while. Some months later he felt another grip on his shoulder, accompanied by an intense feeling of welcome. When he told the locals about his experience they said it was the ghost of an old lady giving him a warm welcome to the Bull Ring.

The Globe Inn

Like the ghost that appears at the Prince Rupert Hotel in Shrewsbury, the Globe has a ghost of an elderly gentleman seen in his nightshirt carrying a brass candlestick and candle glowing in the dark.

A businessman was finding it hard to sleep in the heat of the room and decided to go for a walk around the town. Being early in the morning, only the night porter was about. He made his way along a corridor to the stairs. Halfway along he saw a man in the nightshirt walking towards him in the middle of the corridor and moved out of his way and said hello. The man did not say a thing as he passed. It was only then that the businessman realised he could see through this apparition. Not surprisingly, he decided not to go for a walk after all!

In the *Shropshire Magazine*, Roma Jones recalls her meeting with the ghost. She was staying at the Globe in 1916 as a child with her parents. One stormy December night she awoke at 2 a.m. and needed the bathroom. Making her way along the dimly-lit landing, the door at the end of the corridor opened. Out came an elderly gentleman with long grey wisps of hair trailing from the sides of his night cap. As he approached she asked who he was, to which he replied, 'It's only me' and continued on his way. She returned to bed puzzled. At breakfast she told her parents who, in turn, asked the waiter about the man upstairs. No one could think who he was. Many years later she learnt that she had encountered the famous Globe ghost.

Being one of the closest buildings to the castle, the Globe was used to house troops when the nearby barracks were full. There is the ghost of a soldier, some believe to be Edward Dobson, who was murdered whilst asleep in 1553. He has been seen on a number of occasions in the old brewhouse on the ground floor and on the stairs. He wears a wig and has a large cloak about his shoulders. Sometimes he is seen with another ghost wearing a round metal helmet and leather jerkin. Several sightings of both men have been seen with one guest seeing the man standing near her bed looking towards her husband. When she put the light on she heard a loud bang in the small dressing room. Bravely she went to see what the noise was and discovered a painting of the castle on the floor with the chain for hanging the picture cut clean through.

One Christmas Eve a large fire roared away in the huge fireplace. Suddenly the door flew open and a gust of freezing wind blew in. Before anyone could get up to close the door a short figure of a male traveller appeared, closing the door behind him with a struggle. The barman asked him what he would like to drink. 'Sherry, a small sherry please my good fellow' the stranger replied. He looked rather pale so the barman told him to go and sit by the fire to warm. The stranger joined the local people and they started to chat. What they thought was odd was not only the style of his clothing, but his constant remarks about the dangers of night travel so far north. This was a time when trains and buses were well-known for safety and punctuality! The stranger went on to tell the group that he was travelling by coach to his daughters for Christmas and had met with problems along the way. One of the reins of his horses had lost a shoe and the coachman had dropped him off at the Globe while he sorted it all out. As the clock struck eight the door once again blew open and the stranger left, followed by the noise of a horse-drawn carriage with horses and slap of leathers. It was only after the stranger had left that people started to wonder what had happened and the barman realised he had not paid for his drink. As he went to clear the glass he noticed a silver coin. It was an old silver coin of 1765 – payment for the sherry and a bonus for Christmas. The stranger caught his coach and the locals all toasted his health and hoped that he made it to his daughters in time.

Broad Street

Many of the houses, including the castle, in Ludlow are owned by the Earl of Powys. One such property in Broad Street has been divided into two four-bedroom houses. It is a fine Georgian town house. The powder room, at the top of the stairs, was used to powder the wigs. Footsteps and noises of the sash windows being raised and lowered are often heard in the left-hand side of the building whilst, on the right-hand side a woman is seen to walk down the stairs and through a blocked door into the other house.

The story behind the haunting is the owner of the property was a cruel man who married his wife for her money. He would often lock her in the powder room for days at a time if she dared to upset him. Is she the middle-aged woman seen walking down the stairs of both houses and pacing in the very small powder room of just 4ft by 4ft? Is she finally trying to escape her cruel husband – perhaps we shall never know.

The Feathers Hotel, Ludlow

This fine example of a sixteenth-century timber-framed building dominates the main street of Ludlow with the splendid carved façade made famous by the film *Four Weddings and a Funeral*

Room 211 has had a number of ghostly sightings and noises, including the sound of frantic clapping followed by hurrying footsteps. One couple experienced a visit from an unseen person who pulled the wardrobe doors open and threw out some of their clothing as they were

The Feathers Hotel.

about to go to sleep. Many guests have said that they have noticed the room would become ice cold and they would feel thin cold fingers run along their backs, followed by an uneasy feeling.

Something very strange happened outside the hotel in 1974. A salesman who had an appointment at the Feathers Hotel had been driving around Ludlow trying to find somewhere to park. A space became available right outside the hotel. In his rush he remembered some papers he needed. Turning back towards his car he saw a beautiful young woman in a miniskirt and a near transparent blouse. What happened next stunned him – she walked straight through his car, stepped onto the pavement and continued to walk right past him. He rushed to the bar and downed a much needed brandy. When the barman asked him what was wrong he explained what he had seen. The barman was not surprised and gave him a drink on the house and told him the background of what he had witnessed. A local paranormal investigator had heard that there had been six sightings of the girl and wanted to know why, in 1974, she was contemporary dressed in a miniskirt. His research pointed to a living woman who, for many years, had visited her favourite aunt at the same time since she had moved there. Suddenly in 1974 the aunt died and the house was sold, but whenever the young woman thought of her aunt she was able to project an image of herself onto the route she used to take. This is believed to be the reason for the Lady in Black making her regular appearance in Bridgnorth.

Ludlow Castle

The well-known story of Ludlow Castle is set in the time of Henry II. A lady of the court, Marion de Bruer, was left in charge of the castle whilst the custodian was away fighting Joce de Dinan. In her boredom she would talk to two prisoners, Walter de Lacy and one of his knights, Arthur, held in the castle by men loyal to Joce. She was a real beauty and took a shine to Arthur. She arranged their escape. A few days later Arthur risked being captured to see Marion again and they became lovers. Not wanting to be found out, she would lower a rope from her bedroom

Ludlow Castle.

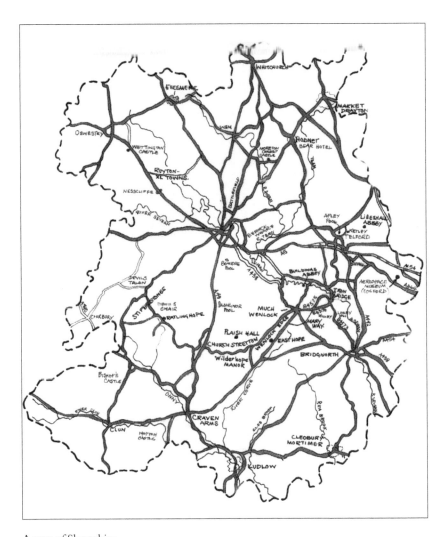

A map of Shropshire.

The churchyard of St Chads, Shrewsbury.

so her lover could join her. One night Arthur persuaded her to take a bath with him. She was always confined to her rooms at night and was never checked on by staff, so they were safe. He climbed the rope and went to her bathroom where she was waiting for him. Whilst they were bathing he had arranged for 100 men to use the rope to seize the castle and kill the garrison. It was not until the next day that Marion realised what her lover had done. She was so distraught at his treachery she rushed to the bedroom and killed her lover with his own sword before throwing herself off the hanging tower, breaking her neck on impact with the rocky outcrop. She is rarely seen. It is believed she only appears if the castle is in danger. In the tower, however, some visitors have felt something rush past them and heard heavy breathing about halfway up the tower – is it Marion or one of her lover's men trying to capture his assailant?

Wheatsheaf Inn, Ludlow

Although never seen, the ghost at the Wheatsheaf is a fun-loving rogue with a wicked sense of humour. If a pretty woman is in the bar, he is known to walk behind them and pinch their bottom, an act which many an unsuspecting and innocent male has been accused of. He also likes messing about with the beer pumps by switching them off or to cause the pressure to build so that the taps would gush unmanned. Before anything happened to the pumps the landlord would hear footsteps in the room above moving from left to right.

As no one has seen him no one is sure who he is – even a medium tried to find out who he was but ended up with riddles rather than names. Could he be one of the officers from the castle who had a secret tunnel to get to the inn for his love of beer and women? He used the tunnel to avoid being caught by his superior officer, who was very religious and had banned his men from entering any place where alcohol was served. By chance, the tunnel was found when checking out the tunnels beneath the castle for munitions' storage. Alternatively, could it be one of the 'lewd and evil disposed persons, rogues, vagabonds, beggars and such like' who frequented the inn during the early 1600s?

four

SHREWSBURY
GHOST WALK

As the main town of Shropshire, Shrewsbury, or Salop as it is sometimes called, has one of the highest numbers of ghosts in the county. There is even a gravestone to my hero, Ebenezer Scrooge, in the rear churchyard of St Chad's overlooking the quarry. This is a prop left over from filming *A Christmas Carol* starring George C. Scott as Scrooge.

> *Start your ghost walk in the heart of the medieval town in Fish Street.*

Fish Street has the great-sounding Grope Lane leading from it and the Bear Steps, all of which form a warren of small lanes, many of which have murderous histories and associated ghosts. The Shuts and Passages are a great way of seeing the town without getting caught up in the modern madness that is now the town centre. They are a series of arteries carrying one through the historic past.

In Fish Street there was once a shop selling shirts and ties called Orriel, run by a Mrs Joyce Jackson who first told of the strange goings on in her shop. While stocktaking after the Christmas rush of late night opening, Mrs Jackson had locked the door and was working in the stock room when she heard someone say something. She was shocked to see a shadow in the shape of a tall male standing by the back wall of the shop. He appeared to be having a conversation with someone. Turning on every light in the shop she watched as the figure by the wall turned away as if talking to someone else and then vanished in front of her. She did not stay too long after that and was soon on her way home. There have been several sightings in the shop by people walking by at night and shop staff.

Could it be the Devil collecting lost souls? On occasions throughout the year the Devil is said to climb the nearby St Alkmund's Church. Built on the hill on which Shrewsbury has developed, St Alkmund's Church has the highest steeple in the town. Here the Devil is said to

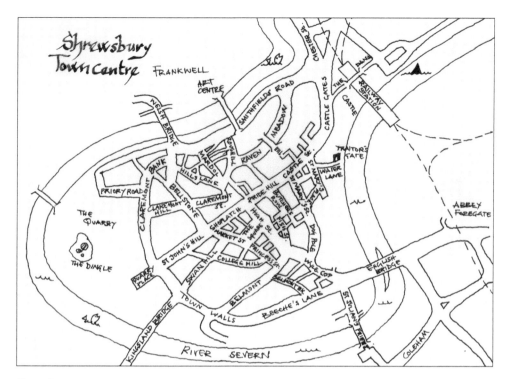

Shrewsbury town map.

look out towards his chair on the Stiperstones. This story was so well-known that a steeplejack drinking his favourite tipple of rum in the Logger Heads pub took the bet that he could climb the steeple and push the Devil off his lookout. Within the hour he was at the top and, with great excitement, waved to the crowd below. He lost his grip and plunged to his death, his back broken on a tomb below. It is claimed that on balmy sunny nights the man is seen climbing the steeple before falling into a waiting cloud just below the base of the steeple.

A few yards from St Alkmund's Church is the now redundant church of St Julian's that re-opened in the 1980s as an art venue, vegetarian café and retail centre for fair trade goods. The owner, Julian (by odd coincidence), lives in the bell tower on three floors. A ghost is said to haunt one of the graves at the front of the church overlooking the Wyle Cop. In the mid-1800s a man was found dead at the nearby Lion Hotel. He was believed to have died in his sleep. With no idea who he was, his effects were used to pay for his burial and he was duly buried one evening.

That night, the watchmen who patrolled the town prior to the peelers all reported hearing howling, screaming and banging coming from the graveyard. The following evening the same gruesome screaming was heard by people walking past the graveyard in a small alley.

It was only when the vicar heard the noise was anything done. Looking at the list of burials, he had the mystery man exhumed, only to find that the poor fellow had not been dead but had suffered from sleeping sickness which merely gives the appearance of death. When the coffin was opened the inside lid was found to be scratched and covered in blood. His fingers were raw to the bone. A terrible look of horror was on his face. The vicar was so shocked by what he

Fish Street with St Alkmund's at the back.

saw that he took himself off to his bed and was not seen for weeks after, and later transferred to another parish. To make sure the man was dead a stake was driven through the heart once the doctor had tested the corpse for vital signs, before being reburied. To this day, the screams of the ill-fated man can be heard late in the evening.

From St Julian's Churchyard turn back up Fish Street that leads to Butchers Row.

In Butchers Row there is a building known as the Abbot's house in which men were billeted during the Civil War. Some people who have visited the building talk of developing breathing difficulty and of feeling as if they are being watched by something not of this world. Others, staying in the Prince Rupert Hotel across the road, speak of seeing ashen faces at the top floor windows looking out across the rooftops.

Across the road, back towards St Alkmund's Church is the Prince Rupert Hotel.

During the civil war the older timber-framed part of the Prince Rupert Hotel, called Jones's Mansion, was used as a base for Prince Rupert. A number of his men lost their lives in battle. In Room 7, there is the ghost of a young man hanging from a beam. It has caused a few people to request another room. Even the staff are not immune to meeting the ghosts and often on early shift in the kitchen or the storeroom they would catch a glimpse of a Civil War soldier going through a sealed-up door.

More recently, when there was filming of *A Christmas Carol* taking place in the town a number of the crew were staying at the hotel. After dinner, three members of the crew were heading off to bed as they had an early start the next day. Joking that they had yet to see a ghost, they saw an elderly gentleman walking towards them in a nightshirt and sleeping cap. A candle was burning in his hand-held candleholder. They moved to one side to let him pass and before they could say anything to him, he smiled and walked through a closed door. They made their 4 a.m. appointment, but only after spending time in the night bar.

From the Prince Rupert Hotel go down Bear Steps, turn left into Fish Street, down Bank Passage, and cross the road through Golden Cross Passage into Princess Street. Ahead of you is No. 25 Princess Street.

In the late sixteenth century, a fire swept through the houses of Milk Street and Princess Street claiming many lives as it quickly spread through the timber-framed buildings. At No. 25 four of the victims were young children burnt to death on the upper floor landing. Their spectres have been seen huddled in a corner. The grief of the mother, who died from smoke inhalation, can be sensed and felt on the landing below as she rushes up the stairs to rescue her children, never to make it.

When the house was rebuilt it saw more tragedy; a man was stabbed to death on the ground floor after a fight in a nearby pub. In the old servants' quarters, next door to the landing where the children died, is seen the ghost of a young woman hanging from the beam. She was a young woman who was treated cruelly after being taken from a poor house as a maid. Such was her torment that her only way to end the pain was to commit suicide.

From Princess Street turn back towards Golden Cross Passage, turning left then right into Wyle Cop and a little way down you will find the Lion Hotel on your right.

The Lion Hotel has a famous ghost seen by many people standing on the balcony in the Adams room. The ghost, dressed in a powder-grey ball gown, glides down the stairs and into the ballroom where she vanishes into thin air. One night porter was so taken aback by seeing a guest vanish in front of him that he left that night and has never set foot in the hotel again. Guests who have been privileged to see her say they feel a sense of peace and tranquillity around her. Mr Astbury, the new owner and a sceptic, was surprised when he was reviewing a new video about the hotel to notice a shape standing in front of the double doors – a lady dressed in grey. Thinking it was a glitch on the tape he asked for a new copy to be made, but the mysterious lady was still there.

The Talbot Bar also has the ghost of a middle-aged man who sits in the corner seat away from the bar, nursing his drink before he attempts to get up, somewhat worse for wear, and then vanishes.

Just down the Wyle Cop from the Lion Hotel is Barrack's Passage.

Barrack's Passage is named after the buildings used as barracks for men fighting alongside Henry Tudor in August 1485. Henry Tudor, later Henry VII, lodged in the timber-framed building on the Wyle Cop, now known as Tudor House. During the 1970s the building was empty when many sightings of men and boys dressed in military uniforms of the Tudor period were reported. Faces have suddenly appeared at the broken windows and dogs will not pass on that side of the passage.

Locally it is believed that the ghosts that appear here are of those who lost their lives on the battlefield at Bosworth. They return to Shrewsbury where they had always been sure of a hearty welcome.

During a recent refurbishment a number of items dating back to the 1400s were found hidden in walls and under old floorboards and removed for safekeeping. The disruption seems to have caused the ghosts to resent the moving of their objects, and they responded by pushing builders around, moving objects and knocking over tools, Many of the objects were returned to the building and as a result, many of the incidents stopped.

> *Retrace your step to Wyle Cop, turn right down the hill cross English Bridge and walk straight ahead to Abbey Foregate.*

Heading out of town down Abbey Foregate is a terrace of three-storey houses where a friendly ghost, Harry, lives. For many years the Griffiths family shared their home with a ghost who would tap and knock in the cellar. Whenever anyone went to investigate the noise would stop. It never happened at night nor on a Sunday. The door to the cellar has a Suffolk latch. Before the noise started the latch was seen to lift, followed by the door opening and closing with the latch returning to the shut position. Within minutes, the knocking would begin. The family enjoyed sharing the house and called the ghost Harry. A later relative who was a boot repairer recognised the noise as someone repairing footwear, and they discovered that a Mr George Bromley worked in the cellar as a cobbler. The family renamed their friendly ghost George when they found out who the cobbler was.

A little way up across the road stands Abbey Lodge guest house. Here there is a ghost in the attic and a second ghost who wanders the lower floors. Strange things started to happen after renovation in 1985. The proprietor, Mr Malloy, felt that he was being watched. He ignored the sensation until one of the builders refused to work after dark because he felt uneasy and remarked that he too felt he was being watched. Later that year a group of visitors from the BBC claimed they had been woken up at 4 a.m. by loud banging and dragging noises from the top floor. Mr Malloy could not account for these interruptions. The top floor was semi-derelict, the staircase padlocked, and no one had been up there for six months. Fearing that an intruder was in the attic he went up with his dog and a friend. Both refused to go past the middle bedroom, the source of the noise. They turned to leave and as they were going downstairs, the footsteps could be heard from within the locked room. Mr Malloy put it down to traffic from the road and went downstairs to begin getting ready for the evening guests. A few days later Mr Malloy's father was visiting and had gone to the nearby public house, the Dun Cow. Returning back to the guest house he looked up to see a face with unkempt grey hair looking out from the attic bedroom. He mentioned this to his son and they decided to investigate further. Taking the keys and accompanied by his dog they went upstairs. Opening the door they could see the bedroom was empty, except for a pair of curtains at the window. These suddenly parted as if someone was drawing them back to look through. Mr Malloy's dog barked once, turned tail and ran off followed by them both in hot pursuit. The following morning, at 3 a.m. Mr Malloy woke to someone shaking the back door of the house. From his bedroom window above the back door he could see no explanation for the violent shaking.

The second ghost at Abbey Lodge is of a housekeeper dressed in grey who is seen carrying a large bunch of keys. The housekeeper suddenly appears in one of the middle-floor bedrooms and is seen to check the linen cupboard before going on her rounds. The daughter of a past landlady was the first to follow this ghost from the bedroom she was sleeping in through to the

Barrack's
Passage.

resident's sitting room. She says she had sat on the lap of the old lady in grey who showed her a bunch of keys.

Further up Abbey Foregate is the Dun Cow Inn which has the ghost of a Dutchman who was executed for the murder of Prince Rupert's steward in the kitchen of the inn. The Dutchman was court marshalled and condemned to death. A scaffold was erected in the stable yard but before the execution, the Dutchman made a short speech. As the rope was put around his neck he said, 'It is grossly unfair that I, a Dutchman, should be executed for killing only one Englishman'. His ghost seems to like upsetting people and making a nuisance of himself. A guest staying at the hotel had been on a tour of the town in the morning with his wife and they had returned for lunch. While in the gent's he saw a tall man dressed in a cavalier's uniform walking out of one of the stalls which amused him and he went about his business with a grin on his face. His grin soon turned to amazement as he turned around and saw the cavalier walk through the side wall. He rushed back to his table and the couple promptly left, leaving without their luggage. Later that day the man telephoned the proprietor, Mr Hayes, and explained what he had seen. He did not want to stay at the inn and explained that his wife would pop in to collect their belongings and pay the bill.

The Dutch cavalier has appeared in the bar and out in the car park – still protesting about the punishment he received at the hands of Prince Rupert and his men.

When Mr Hayes took over the pub he was not aware of the ghost stories. One morning the whole family overslept, and when they looked at the clocks in the pub – be they wind up, battery or mains electric – they had all stopped at 6.45 a.m., the time the execution was believed to have taken place. The family have seen someone on the first floor described as a monk who walks along the front of the building and through the walls.

During some renovation work in the bar area which required workmen to work after the inn was closed, they often heard someone walk across the wooden floor from left to right, and back again, along the front of the building on the first floor. This went on for a few nights. One night they apologised for the noise they were making and for keeping a member of the family awake. They told the proprietor what they had heard. He took them upstairs to the front of the Dun Cow to show that there was no physical way anyone could walk along the front of the building. There were three walls across the route and the floors were carpeted. They left quickly and after that would only work in pairs at night.

The last sighting of the monk was in 2003 and the Dutch cavalier seems to have moved on, as he has not been seen since. The present proprietor has heard noises but not seen anything and lives in hope that all will remain quiet.

From the Dun Cow walk back towards the town centre over the English Bridge and up the Wyle Cop where you will find the Nags Head Inn on your right.

During renovation at the Nags Head Inn in 1982, workmen discovered a secret room. It served no useful purpose in the renovation and the space was resealed. Since that time there have been heard footsteps and sounds of heavy breathing coming from the secret space. On three occasions these have been accompanied with loud crashing noises that have been violent

The Dun Cow Inn.

enough to set off the burglar alarm. Lights have frequently been turned on and off and the jukebox has been known to suddenly spring into life.

There is a more sinister story at the Nags Head Inn. High up in one of the attic rooms can be found a small cupboard. On the back of the door is a crude painting of an old prophet. It is said that if anyone should look upon the image they would surely go mad. Indeed, this may have been the reason for the deaths of three people who have lodged the night. The first was a coachman in the mid-1700s who had just landed a prestigious job with the local lord and had been seen celebrating his good fortune in the bar. When he did not appear in the morning, the landlord went upstairs to find him hanging from a beam in the room. Could he be the tall man in a long coat seen walking the corridors at night?

The second death was of a young lady, elated by her recent engagement and excited by her wedding plans. Her fiancée was going to take her to meet his parents. On retiring to her room people heard screams just before she threw herself out of the window and under the wheels of a coach – she was crushed to death.

Finally an army officer, a survivor of the trenches of the First World War, was found shot dead with his own service revolver opposite the open cupboard door.

After that incident, the room was finally sealed shut. People passing through the darkened alley that runs alongside the Nags Head Inn often report seeing the flicker of candlelight moving about in the closed room.

From the Nags Head Inn continue up the Wyle Cop and turn right into Dogpole. A few yards up the hill can be found Ye Olde House.

Ye Olde House was the family home of the Rocke family and it was here that the Princess Mary Tudor stayed in 1526 on her way to Ludlow Castle. Mary Tudor, later Mary I, held court at Ludlow Castle for approximately eighteen months when she was only ten years old.

Ye Olde House passed from the Rocke family to the Peele family with the last in line being Miss E.J. Peele who left the house and contents to the Shrewsbury Civic Society.

A ghostly figure surrounded by a glowing mist has been seen on several occasions by Miss Peele and others. This ghostly figure has been seen to go into the cellar from where the enticing smell of fried bacon wafts. The sound of chopping wood is sometimes heard, along with whispering voices and footsteps along the corridors of the house. A little child has been seen behind a large plant pot, crouching down as if playing hide and seek.

Continue up Dogpole and turn right into St Marys Place. Ahead of you to the Parade Shopping Centre.

The Parade Shopping Centre is built on the site of a former mansion and the old Royal Shrewsbury Infirmary. The Parade has a number of ghosts, many of which are believed to be members of a dedicated nursing team returning to their old hospital.

The most reported sighting is that of the matron. Tall, thin and with an air of authority, the matron glides along the shopping mall in what would have been a hospital ward. She is seen to disappear into the rooms once used as the hospital kitchens. It is also here that a Mr Wood of Shrewsbury, and many others, have reported the ghost of a scruffy man standing by the old door of the soup kitchen. He is seen for a few seconds before disappearing.

A nurse is said to walk through the areas that were once operating theatres, now luxury apartments, and appears to check instruments and invisible oxygen bottles. Another nurse, seen at the foot of the stairs dressed in the uniform of the First World War period, is seen to look up, smile, and then vanish.

The final ghost is that of a nurse dressed in a white uniform. She is no longer seen but nursing staff who served at the Infirmary when it was open reported seeing her vision appearing at the end of the beds of patients who would die in their sleep that night.

At night, screams, moans and cries echo throughout the Parade Shopping Centre and yet bring no sense of harm to the security people on duty.

From the front of the Parade Shopping Centre continue down St Marys Place. As you approach Castle Street there is a lane to you right called St Mary's Water Lane which leads down to Traitors Gate.

On 22 February 1645, Captain John Benbow changed allegiance and allowed Parliamentary troops to enter and capture Shrewsbury Castle. During the English Civil War, Benbow served in the Parliamentary Army, and later crossed over to the Royalist side. He was court-martialled as a traitor at Chester, and was shot at Shrewsbury in the garden under the Castle Mount.

His body was left hanging on Traitors Gate as a deterrent to other would-be turncoats. People walking down the lane, or along the river footpath, sometimes look up to see the skeletal remains hanging from the archway. The gates have long since gone, with just the opening to the river standing.

Retrace your steps in to Castle Street and turn right to Shrewsbury Castle.

Shrewsbury Castle was originally an Anglo-Saxon timber fortification guarding the only dry-shod approach to the town. The Norman castle, built of red sandstone, was founded by Roger de Montgomery in around 1070. During the summer of 1138, King Stephen laid siege and captured the fortress, which was held by William FitzAlan for the Empress Maud. Apart from the gateway very little of the Norman building survives. Much of it was demolished during the rebuilding and strengthening of the castle by Edward I in around 1300, when an outer bailey was added.

The castle is built on the site of an earlier wooden structure said to have been occupied by the notorious villain, Bloundi Jack, or Bloody Jack as he has become known. Bloundi Jack has been seen on the lawns in front of the castle dragging a screaming naked woman by her hair, followed by a group of shadowy figures.

In the tenth century, Bloundi Jack would lure innocent young female victims with the promise of marriage and riches to his abode, whereupon he would imprison and rape them repeatedly. In a final act of cruelty he would cut off their fingers and toes before throwing them to the wicked ways of his followers. When they had tired of their sport, their victim would have her throat cut and be thrown into the watery grave of the river.

In due course, the townspeople got to hear of these diabolical murders and raided the wooden castle and captured Bloundi Jack. He denied all knowledge of the murders, blaming his men. As one was being led to the gallows he shouted to the baying crowd that Bloundi Jack kept tokens of his victims in his room. Following a search, the rotting fingers and toes of twenty-four women were found. Such was their anger at the fate of these innocents that Bloundi Jack was bound, tied, and drawn behind a horse to the top of Wyle Cop to be hanged,

Shrewsbury Castle.

drawn and quartered, for all to see. His head was put on a pike outside the castle walls and the rest of his body thrown to the depths of the River Severn.

> **From the grounds of the Castle turn right into Castle Gates and then into the railway station.**

Shrewsbury's railway station is the gateway to Wales and the north. A ghostly Shrewsbury Councillor has made the same journey to Platform Three since 1887. During a particularly heavy fall of snow he was driven up on to the platform in a horse-drawn hackneyed carriage. While waiting for his train to arrive, part of the cast iron and glass roof collapsed under the weight of the heavy snow, crushing him to death and injuring horse and driver. A man's shadowy figure stands and sometimes sits near the ramp entrance from Castle Gates and is seen to check his pocket watch while looking up the track for the train he was never to catch.

A hooded figure, possibly a monk, appears from the underground service tunnel and has been seen by people leaving the station after the last train has left.

> **Leaving the station behind and heading toward the town centre, a few hundred yards on the right is the original site of Shrewsbury School, now the library and local record office.**

The grey lady is known to walk in this building, checking up on things as she walks. She has been seen by cleaners at night and in the early morning in the book store. A security guard called in response to an alarm was surprised when he saw her walk through a rack of books, emerging on the other side before turning and vanishing. The building on Castle Gates was once the home of Shrewsbury School which is now over the river at Kingsland. Is the woman one of the matrons checking up on her charges, or is it a wife of one of the past masters of the school?

> **Further up the street is the site of the former Peter Dominic's wine merchants.**

Since 1972, when the shop was opened, a number of staff kept saying to the manager that they heard someone moving around upstairs in the stock room. Every time the manager investigated nothing was found. Just before Christmas 1972 one of the assistants, Mrs Panitz, had to take a few boxes of glasses up to the storeroom. As she walked past the room where the noises came from she saw the figure of a man standing by the window. He seemed to be wearing a blue suit and had short hair. She thought it was one of her work colleagues having a crafty fag but when she went downstairs, she found all the staff serving customers. She told her colleagues what she had just seen and they rushed upstairs, thinking it was an intruder stealing the cigarettes stored there. No one was found and no one was seen or heard running away. She mentioned

The Old Police House.

the incident to her friend who worked next door, who told her that often after Dominic's had closed she had heard noises coming from their side and had seen a man wearing a blue suit standing in the first-floor window looking down the street.

Opposite St Marys Place, on the right, is a little alleyway leading to the Old Police House and gaol.

During the late 1890s a policeman was found hanging in one of the cells of the Old Police House, his hands were trapped between the rope and his neck. Some believe he had committed suicide, but had second thoughts and had tried to pull the cord away to save his neck. Others believe a local gang who had been making threats against him carried out a murder. Nothing was ever proved. He is frequently seen in the holding cell or standing close to the entrance of the building, either as head and shoulders only or as a uniformed figure without the helmet, trying to say something which is never heard.

Across the lane is the old gaol. This is the home of a very mischievous spirit who walks various items of stationery across the main upper hall. Once the offices for the constabulary, it is now general offices. Many items, including a roll of sellotape, moved down the centre of the office a few feet off he ground and onto a desk at the opposite end of the room.

Walk back out of the lane and turn right into Pride Hill. On the right is WH Smith.

This was once the tearoom and dance hall of the Morris's café where people often met their loved ones. Built for the Pride family, remnants of the eleventh-century stone town walls can be seen in the basement where a hooded figure has been seen. Upstairs a beautiful young woman appears, but beware – she has a nasty habit of decaying before your very eyes. Footsteps can be heard in the old ballroom on the first floor and members of staff have reported hearing many strange noises including music and singing when working in the stock room that was the tea room.

> **Go down the hill to Shoplatch and turn left into Draytons Passage.**

Alongside Draytons Passage is the Hole in the Wall and the Mardol Vaults Inn. The Mardol Vaults Inn is locally nicknamed the Blood Tub due to the number of fights that often break out. During refurbishment in the 1980s, the remains of a stone mansion built in 1325 were uncovered. The fine, carved stone window frames now form part of the interior decoration and were possibly part of the palace of the Princess of Powys.

A young female, Lady Sarah, makes after-hour visits to the main bar in the Mardol Vaults. She smiles as she walks through a modern wall. A barmaid was so upset by the experience that she promptly handed in her notice, never to return as guest or employee. Lady Sarah was the daughter of the Shutt family who held high office in Shrewsbury. She died in the fourteenth century in tragic circumstances, having arranged to meet her lover from a rival Welsh family in the old St Chad's Churchyard. Her family found out about the intended rendezvous and were so vexed that their only choice of punishment was to starve Sarah to death in the cellar. As for her lover, no records exist of his downfall although the Shutt family were known to quickly dispatch anyone who threatened their position.

> **From here walk down the hill to Shoplatch and turn right into Bellstone.**

Looming out of the car park ahead is a black and white timber-framed building, Rowley's House, which is now the local Shropshire history museum. Two ghostly costumed figures share this timber-framed building. The first is a fine lady seen to rest upon the four-poster bed displayed upstairs. Some believe she is the wife of Sir Vincent Corbet, who died in childbirth. The bed was given by the Corbet family to the museum. It had never been unpacked because it's intended home at Moreton Corbet Castle was never finished.

The second visitor seems oblivious to the existence of the above lady, despite being in costume of a similar period. When the house was in private ownership in the 1800s there were often reports from servants and owners of a ghost walking upstairs and along the corridors in search of something. He does not evoke fear or alarm. When locking up at night members of the museum staff have spoken of feeling as if someone is walking behind them, but upon turning round no one is there. They say it feels as if someone is guarding over their safety.

> *Walk back toward Bellstone turning up Claremont Hill. Turn left onto Claremont bank where St Chad's Church can be found on the left.*

Since early medieval times there has been a church in Shrewsbury dedicated to St Chad, first Bishop of Mercia in the seventh century. By the end of the eighteenth century, the large but ageing building had fallen into disrepair and cracks had appeared in the tower. The great engineer, Thomas Telford, advised that it was in danger of collapse – and he was right. One morning in 1788 the parishioners awoke to find they had a pile of rubble.

After much argument a new site was found on the derelict town wall. Stones from old St Chad's were used as foundations and the foundation stone was laid on St Chad's Day, 2 March 1790.

The film crew from *A Christmas Carol* used an old grave stone and had it rewritten with the name 'Ebenezer Scrooge' on it. It makes a great photo opportunity for any ghost hunter.

> *Across the road is an open area locally known as the Quarry.*

The dingle is a small sunken area with a delightful floral display designed by such great gardeners as Percy Thrower. The area was used in the 1600s to burn witches and murderers. One victim of burning at the stake was a Mrs Foxall, who murdered her husband after he beat her. She broke loose from her burning stake and ran screaming towards the townsfolk in flames. On the anniversary of her death, in November 1647, she is seen to run past the Dingle heading towards St John's Hill.

> *From the Quarry walk across the green to Quarry Place and turn right on to Town Walls. After Swan Hill you will see the old stone tower (now a private house) which is haunted by two children burned to death in the Great Fire in the late sixteenth century. From here walk down Bellmont and turn left into Princess Street. The first shutt (passage) on your right is Golden Cross Passage, next to which stands the Golden Cross Inn.*

The Golden Cross Inn dates back to 1428 and is reputed to be the oldest existing public house in Shrewsbury. It also claims to be the oldest to hold a continuous licence in the country. Its original name was the Sextry, so-called because it was originally the sacristy of Old St Chad's Church. Similarly, the original name of Golden Cross Passage was Sextry Shutt. In 1933 a couple of timber-framed archways were discovered which a local archaeologist dated back to the time of Henry III. The Golden Cross Inn was used as Royalist retreat during the Civil War.

After refurbishment in 1975, some guests and staff have felt a sense of being watched and have seen a monk, kneeling as if in prayer, and no doubt connected to the time when the building was used as a sacristy. The monk has also been seen fighting off an invisible foe as he tries to protect what little silver was left in the church after the raids during the Civil War.

> *Retrace your steps to Market Street where the remains of the old Music Hall can be seen.*

At the old Music Hall a ghostly dandy has often been seen off stage right, flicking his face with a large handkerchief – this is taken by the cast as a good sign that the production will work. The Music Hall closed in 2009 after 169 years, and the building is now home to a cinema.

BIBLIOGRAPHY

Books

McCarthy, Christine (1988), *Some Ghostly Tales of Shropshire*
Neal, Toby (2007), *Shropshire Since 1900*
Hughes, Jean (1977), *Shropshire Folklore, Ghosts and Witchcraft*
Brooks, John (1994), *The Good Ghost Guide*
Haining, Peter (1982), *The Dictionary of Ghosts*
Hole, Christina (1990), *Haunted England*
Spencer, John & Anne (1998), *The Ghost Handbook*
Harper, Charles G. (1907), *Haunted Houses*
Underwood, Peter (1996), *Ghosts and Haunted Places*
Underwood, Peter (1971), *A-Z of British Ghosts*

Newspapers & Magazines:

Shropshire Magazine
Shropshire Star
Shrewsbury Chronicle

Also information from reports on the following:

BBC Radio Shropshire and website.
BBC Midlands Today
Beacon Radio 303

Other titles published by The History Press

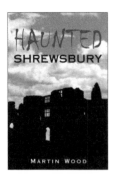

Haunted Shrewsbury
MARTIN WOOD

From accounts of poltergiests to first-hand encounters with ghouls, this collection of tales compiled by Shrewsbury's illustrious town crier contains a chilling range of ghostly goings-on. Drawing on historical and contemporary sources, it relates Shrewsbury's more mysterious and murky history. This phenomenal gathering of spooks and spectres will captivate anyone interested in the supernatural history of the area.

978 0 7524 4303 4

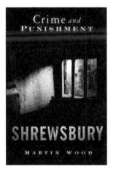

Crime and Punishment: Shrewsbury
MARTIN WOOD

This light-hearted yet well-researched exploration of punishments handed down in Shrewsbury over the centuries features tales of criminals and their misdeeds from the Romans to the last execution to take place in Shrewsbury in 1960. The stories of these criminals, from Thomas Hughes who was whipped for stealing a turkey, to Josiah Mister who was hanged for attacking the wrong man are bound to captivate anyone interested in Shrewsbury's shadowy past.

978 0 7524 4546 5

Haunted Birmigham
ARTHUR SMITH AND RACHEL BANNISTER

From creepy happenings in the city centre to stories of phantoms in theatres, pubs and hospitals, this book contains a chilling range of ghostly tales. Drawing on historical and conetmporary sources, the authors tell of a landlady who haunts her old pub, two dead workmen who came back to haunt the town hall and an ex-mayor who still watches over the city.

978 0 7524 4017 0

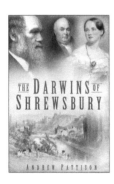

The Darwins of Shrewsbury
ANDREW PATTISON

Many people have written biographies of Charles Darwin, but the story of his family and roots in Shrewsbury is little known. This book, containing original research, fills that gap. It is fully illustrated with contemporary and modern pictures, and will be of interest to anyone wanting to discover more about the development of Shrewsbury's most famous son.

978 0 7524 4867 1

Visit our website and discover thousands of other History Press books.
www.thehistorypress.co.uk